T0275059

Ed Garvey Unvarnished

ED GARVEY
UNVARNISHED

Lessons from a Visionary Progressive

ROB ZALESKI

The University of Wisconsin Press

Publication of this book has been made possible, in part, through support from the Anonymous Fund of the College of Letters and Science at the University of Wisconsin–Madison.

The University of Wisconsin Press
728 State Street, Suite 443
Madison, Wisconsin 53706-1428
uwpress.wisc.edu

Gray's Inn House, 127 Clerkenwell Road
London ECR 5DB, United Kingdom
eurospanbookstore.com

Printed in the United States of America

This book may be available in a digital edition.

Library of Congress Cataloging-in-Publication Data
Names: Garvey, Ed, 1940-2017, interviewee. | Zaleski, Rob (Journalist), author, interviewer.
Title: Ed Garvey unvarnished: lessons from a visionary progressive / Rob Zaleski.
Description: Madison, Wisconsin: The University of Wisconsin Press, [2019] | Foreword by David Maraniss.
Identifiers: LCCN 2019008126 | ISBN 9780299323707 (cloth: alk. paper)
Subjects: LCSH: Garvey, Ed, 1940-2017—Interviews. | Politicians—Wisconsin—Interviews. | Political activists—Wisconsin—Interviews.
| Progressivism (United States politics).
| Wisconsin—Politics and government—21st century.
| United States—Politics and government—21st century.
| LCGFT: Interviews.
Classification: LCC F586.42.G37 A4 2019 | DDC 977.5/044092—dc23
LC record available at https://lccn.loc.gov/2019008126

To my dad, Eugene Zenon Zaleski, the fastest man
in Kentucky and the greatest motivator I've known

Martin Luther King Jr.

Our lives begin to end the day we become silent
about things that matter.

Contents

David Maraniss

Foreword

Ed Garvey was a small *d* democrat to the end, a man who believed there was no stronger act of patriotism than dissent against the established order when he saw injustice—and he saw more than enough injustice to keep him busy all his life. He loved nothing more than taking on powerful interests in his home state of Wisconsin and across the American landscape: Billionaire owners in the National Football League who treated players like disposable parts. Rapacious mineral mining companies that sought to profit from and pollute the natural bounty of his home state. Wealthy donors who subverted the electoral process and bought access with massive campaign contributions. His goal might have been to comfort the afflicted, but his pleasure came in afflicting the comfortable.

The "kid from Burlington" was also a big *D* Democrat who twice ran for public office at the top of the party ticket for the U.S. Senate in 1986 and for governor in 1998. He was the underdog both times and lost both times. From there he reoriented himself to a role in which he was more comfortable, prodding and poking the powers that be whenever and however he could as a modern-day incarnation of his Wisconsin hero, Bob La Follette. His annual Fighting Bob Fest served as the rallying point for progressive forces as the state and nation lurched between darkness and light, fear and hope, past and future. It is perhaps fitting that he died in February 2017, at the dawn of the Trump era, which represented everything he detested, but too bad he did not live to see Wisconsin restore its progressive traditions by finally disposing of its union-busting governor, Scott Walker.

Everything about him—the little *d*, the big *D*, the progressive—made it appropriate for Garvey's story to be revived and explained, in his own words and those of people who knew him, by a journalist who worked for years at Madison's progressive newspaper, *The Capital Times*. Rob Zaleski does not hide his admiration for his subject, even as he maintains a reporter's distance. Zaleski, who for a crucial period at *The Capital Times* was under the editorial tutelage of my father, Elliott Maraniss, is not the sort of writer who panders to politicians. So it is a meaningful testament that Garvey earned his respect more than anyone he wrote about in his long and distinguished career. And readers will notice in their many interviews that there is no retreating from difficult themes, from Garvey's political misjudgments and frequent disdain for the caution of fellow Democrats to his personal grudges to his slow demise from Parkinson's disease.

Garvey was always pushing for more, from himself and his party, even his family. Barbara Lawton, his running mate in the gubernatorial race, recalled for me a time when one of her sons asked one of Garvey's daughters what it was like growing up with him as a parent and she responded something akin to, "Well, he'd kick us into the corner and say, 'Come out when you read the *New York Times*.'" He had a caustic wit, thrived on gallows humor, yet this book reflects his life in that his words are infused with optimism. He would never give up and never relinquish his belief that the people would prevail. And he had an irresistible energy that drew others to him. Mark Murphy, reflecting the view of others who wrote testimonials of Garvey, called him "one of the most engaging, outgoing people I'd ever met."

The fact that Murphy would effusively praise Garvey says just about everything you need to know about him. Murphy is the president of the Green Bay Packers and, in that role, hangs out with NFL owners who congenitally despise people like Garvey and his successors who have run the NFL Players Association. But Murphy, who works for a team where the people are the owners, has always been more sympathetic to players than his muckety-muck cohort, a sentiment that started when he was a player rep during his days with the Washington Redskins. Murphy said Garvey not only "made everything fun," even during the two player strikes he orchestrated in 1974 and 1982, but he was great at bringing people together and holding them together to reach a common goal. Garvey took his job with the players association when he was only thirty-one, at a time when it was weak and unrecognized, and he led the movement that gave players more freedom. As Dave Zirin wrote in *The Nation* when he learned of Garvey's death, "There would not be a union for NFL players—quite literally, without the fighting political spirit of Ed Garvey."

It was through Garvey's work with the players union that Zaleski first dealt with him. Zaleski was the sports editor of a strike paper in Green Bay in 1974 when the players first went on strike against the owners, and his little paper kept breaking stories that the big city dailies missed because they were getting leaks from a knowledgeable source who trusted them—striker to striker. That source was Ed Garvey. One could say that this book is his biggest leak, his own story, a story that is big, generous, cantankerous, illuminating, joyful, dark, sniping, often right, sometimes wrong, rarely in doubt, and always on the side of the powerless. Here is the Fighting Ed Fest.

Preface

In my thirty-plus years in the newspaper business, there was no one I came to respect more than Ed Garvey. That's saying a lot. As a sportswriter, then a reporter, and finally as a news columnist for *The Capital Times* in Madison, Wisconsin—where I spent the last twenty-six years of my career—I'm guessing I interviewed about ten thousand people from all walks of life.

Though we weren't friends—as a rule, I never socialized with people I wrote about—I interviewed Ed perhaps a dozen times over those three decades. The first time was in the early 1970s, over the phone, when he was the young, brash executive director of the new—and much despised—National Football League Players Association (NFLPA), and I was the young, brash sports editor of the *Green Bay Daily News*, a fledgling and sometimes reckless daily started by striking printers from the *Green Bay Press-Gazette*. While our circulation was barely twelve thousand—or about one-fourth that of the *Press-Gazette*—we had gained a certain amount of credibility by breaking several big stories leading up to the NFLPA's strike in 1974.

Unbeknownst to all but a few people, including most staffers at the *Daily News,* our source for those scoops was none other than Garvey himself, who would call our sports department—usually John Finkler, my assistant, who later worked for the University of Wisconsin athletic department—from the union's headquarters in Washington, DC. (Years later, Garvey would often say there were only two media voices that gave the union a fair shake in its rocky first few years: Red Smith, the legendary sports columnist for the *New York Times,* and the now defunct *Green Bay Daily News.*)

Why the great and enduring respect? I admired Garvey's intellect and, once he entered the political arena in the 1980s, his willingness to chastise even fellow Democrats if he felt they weren't living up to the party's ideals. I admired his piercing wit—though I'd undoubtedly feel differently if I'd been the target of one of his zingers—and the fact that, unlike many public figures, he was quick to acknowledge his own shortcomings.

I admired the role that he and his law firm, Garvey & Stoddard, S.C., played in three of the most impressive—and implausible—grassroots environmental victories I've ever witnessed: Exxon's failed attempt to build a zinc and copper mine at the headwaters of the pristine Wolf River in northeastern Wisconsin; Adams County's refusal to allow multinational Perrier Inc. to build a giant bottling plant that would have threatened underground springs in the town of New Haven, near Wisconsin Dells; and the tiny Town of Porter's success in blocking a factory farm from being built in its community in eastern Rock County.

And then, of course, there was the lawsuit Garvey helped win that led to more humane treatment of inmates at the supermax state prison (now called the Wisconsin Secure Program Facility) near Boscobel. And his intervention in the state's enormous settlement with tobacco companies, which significantly reduced the amount law firms could be paid for working on those cases.

Most of all, I admired Garvey's unwavering optimism despite three failed attempts at public office and some daunting challenges in his personal life. One of Ed and Betty Garvey's three adult daughters, Lizzie, has severe autism. And, in 2008, at age 68, Ed was diagnosed with Parkinson's disease—which would eventually take his life in 2017.

All of which explains, in large part, why I sought out Garvey in late November 2010, a few weeks after the Republican Party's startling success in that year's midterm elections—an eye-opening and unnerving tsunami that included the election of pugnacious conservative Scott Walker as Wisconsin's governor, and, even more baffling, the defeat of Wisconsin Senator Russ Feingold, a nationally esteemed maverick Democrat, by a coy and mysterious Tea Party candidate named Ron Johnson.

Still shell-shocked and unable to make sense of it, I was driving one morning and happened to hear Garvey being interviewed on Wisconsin Public Radio—and a light bulb flashed in my head. I hadn't seen Ed since 2008, when he called to express his sympathy after I was downsized out of my job at *The Capital Times*. Misery loves company, he'd mused in that phone call, noting that he'd recently gotten the bombshell about his Parkinson's but quickly adding that he was expected to have just minor symptoms for at least the next couple years.

I knew Ed was still active at his environmental law firm, based in Madison, and writing a provocative daily blog on the progressive FightingBob.com website that he'd created in 2001 in honor of Wisconsin's own "Fighting" Bob La Follette, unarguably the most influential progressive politician in U.S. history. He also organized a rousing political rally each

September—dubbed Fighting Bob Fest—that attracted thousands of mostly gray-haired lefties to the fairgrounds in
Baraboo, forty miles north of Madison, to hear some of the
biggest names in left-wing politics, including Bernie Sanders
and Jesse Jackson. (The event moved to Madison in 2011 and is
now held in Milwaukee and La Crosse as well.)

But I could tell from the tone of his voice in the radio interview that he was apoplectic over the midterm results and ready
to do battle. Perhaps, I surmised as I turned up the volume and
drove slowly through the University of Wisconsin Arboretum,
Garvey and I could collaborate on a book—one that would re-
instill hope in demoralized souls like me.

My idea for the book, which crystallized over the next few
days, was fairly straightforward. I strongly felt it should not
be a political book per se—one that focused on policy issues
or ideology and was aimed at political scholars and other so-
called experts—but a book that was accessible, engrossing, and,
yes, entertaining. A book, in other words, that would appeal
to the masses of Americans from all backgrounds who had
lifted Barack Obama to victory in 2008. I also felt it should offer
a blueprint of sorts for disillusioned Americans seeking a way
out of this right-wing onslaught.

To that end, I decided it would incorporate two central
themes: What, in Garvey's view, would Fighting Bob La Follette, who helped rescue America from the railroad and lum-
ber barons and other corporate interests who controlled the
reins of power in the early 1900s, have done if confronted with
the political situation that exists today? And, along with that,
Garvey's reflections on the highs and lows of his own remarkable life; more specifically, how a kid from a conservative farm
town in southeast Wisconsin, with aspirations of becoming a
star golfer, evolved into a liberal activist and a prominent,

unflinching voice of the far left and—even more important—a champion of society's underdogs.

In addition, I wanted to explore how this sensitive and prideful man was coping with the frightening realization that, because of Parkinson's, he was facing a slow, agonizing decline in both his mental and physical capacities. So in that respect, the framework would be somewhat similar to that utilized by author Mitch Albom in his deeply moving book *Tuesdays with Morrie*. That was my hope anyway.

I also felt that, since it wasn't an actual biography, a no frills question-and-answer format would work best. Much like a *60 Minutes* or Bill Moyers interview—or, if you will, the often controversial and highly popular *Playboy* magazine interviews of a bygone era—I figured it would capture Garvey's full persona and allow him to elaborate on issues he believed were most pertinent. At the same time, it would allow me to press him on issues I felt were being underplayed or, in some cases, ignored by the mainstream media and leaders of both parties.

I also made it clear that I wasn't interested in doing a book that exaggerated his accomplishments or anointed him for sainthood. He might not like some of the questions, I cautioned, and he would have no censorship rights once the interviews were over. He actually seemed relieved by that—although I did witness the infamous Garvey temper on several occasions.

When I broached the idea over lunch in late November 2010, Garvey's eyes lit up. "When do you want to start?" he asked excitedly. He agreed it would be fun—even cathartic—to meet one-on-one every three or four weeks to hash out the burning issues in these troubled times. He was still putting in full-time hours at his law firm, but he would find the time, he assured me. (Three months later, while vacationing in Zihuata-nejo, Mexico, my wife Cindy and I were shocked by TV reports of mammoth protests on Madison's Capitol Square against Scott Walker's anti-union crusade. I emailed Garvey and asked, "Seriously, what do you think Fighting Bob would do in a situation like this?" His quick response: "Probably move to Mexico.")

The first of our seventeen interview sessions—which ranged from sixty to ninety minutes, depending on Garvey's mood or the constraints of his schedule—took place on a clear but brutally cold morning in February 2011. We sat at a small, square table in the study of his elegant seven-bedroom Georgian-style home that sat atop a hill in the heart of leafy Shorewood Hills, an old, traditional upper-crust community that leans Democratic and is just down the road from the University of Wisconsin campus. (In 2013, he and Betty moved to a condo on Madison's west side.)

The setting proved ideal. Over the next six months we got together every week or two in the same spot, with Ed usually clad in a polo shirt, khakis, and gym shoes—often after he'd just returned home from a Zumba class, which eased much of the stiffness associated with his Parkinson's disease—and sipping a cup of hot coffee. When the weather finally turned pleasant in June, we moved to his favorite room in the entire house, a large screened-in porch surrounded by a yard of brilliant flowers and songbirds that was right out of a Monet painting.

Ed Garvey, I concluded after that last interview, was a flawed but honorable and brutally honest man, much as I'd assumed. And behind the confrontational façade, a kind, compassionate man and a fierce, uncompromising fighter for the have-nots.

So why, readers may ask, did I wait till now to publish this book? Because in our final meeting, Ed mentioned he was also working on a book on his NFLPA days and hoped to complete it by the end of the year. That caught me by surprise, and after we discussed it further, we agreed that, as colorful and widely known as he was, there probably wasn't a market for two books on Ed Garvey.

So I dropped my book idea and set my notes aside—until Garvey's death in 2017. I was vacationing in Mexico again when I got the news and, thus, did not attend the funeral. However, I was amazed by the many glowing tributes to him—including a long obit in the *New York Times*—which made me realize that Garvey had truly left his mark and would be remembered as one of the most dynamic and compelling figures in Wisconsin's storied history. It also dawned on me that in this rancorous era of Scott Walker and Donald Trump—and with the Democratic Party still in the midst of an identity crisis—disillusioned progressives could benefit from his visionary perspective and, perhaps, using his rough blueprint, find a path that would help unite ordinary Americans to a common cause. Much as Fighting Bob had done more than a century earlier.

To be sure, much has changed since 2011—and not in a positive way. In fact, most of the issues Ed and I discussed are still major concerns today and, in many cases, have been exacerbated by Walker, Trump, and their ilk. So I think readers will not only find the interviews relevant but extremely valuable in devising a strategy for the future.

What follows is the edited transcripts of those interviews: unvarnished, vintage Ed Garvey—blunt, humorous, thought-provoking, acerbic, bitingly sarcastic. But never dull. Not surprisingly, he answered every question I tossed at him and agreed that nothing would be off the record. In fact, he was taken aback just twice during those seventeen sessions. The first was when I suggested that some critics would describe his sense of humor as caustic, even mean-spirited at times. Caustic he could accept, but mean-spirited? That was never his intent, he said with a wounded expression.

He also balked when, in our final session, I asked if he believed in God and a hereafter. He didn't want to go there, he said dismissively with a wave of his hand, but finally relented after I noted with a laugh that it was the only time he'd avoided a question in the six months we'd been getting together.

Turns out he did believe in a supreme being—sort of. You'll have to read the book.

Ed Garvey Unvarnished

1

CRUSHING THE UNIONS

On the morning of our first meeting, Ed Garvey eagerly greeted me at the front door of his home and couldn't wait to begin. Like most people in Wisconsin, he was stunned by what had occurred the day before, on Friday, February 11. Newly elected governor Scott Walker had unveiled a sweeping budget repair bill that would remove nearly all collective bargaining rights for the majority of public employees and make it easier for employers to fire workers involved in any form of union unrest. It was nothing less than a blatant attempt to crush organized labor in Wisconsin.

Not only that, but Walker maintained that anyone who didn't see this coming must have been in a coma. "This is not a shock," he asserted. "The shock would be if we didn't go forward with this." (The *Milwaukee Journal-Sentinel* later reported that an investigation of his speeches showed that the governor had never publicly mentioned the details of his draconian strategy on the campaign trail.)

But as appalled and incensed as he was by what he and others perceived as a ruthless power grab, Garvey calmly pointed out over the next ninety minutes that this was merely the latest in a series of assaults on middle- and low-income Americans that had its roots in the 1980 election of Ronald Reagan.

Garvey noted that he and other progressive leaders such as Bernie Sanders and the late Senator Paul Wellstone of Minnesota had been warning about the long-term consequences for years, but few people listened or seemed to care. Now, perhaps, his fellow Democrats and other working-class Americans would finally wake up, he sighed. The only question: was it too late?

●

ROB ZALESKI: OK, I admit it. I'm absolutely bewildered. Just two years after Bush and the Republicans took us to the brink of a second Great Depression, voters have essentially—as Barack Obama put it—given the keys back to the same people who drove our economy into the ditch.

More demoralizing yet, Wisconsin voters have elected a conservative Republican, Scott Walker, as governor and ousted Democratic Senator Russ Feingold, one of the most widely respected senators in the entire country, and replaced him with a Tea Party guy, Ron Johnson. And yesterday, Walker announced his shocking plan to essentially destroy Wisconsin's public employee unions. How did we get to this point?

ED GARVEY: Well, first of all, it didn't just happen. When I woke up the morning after the midterms, I was only surprised with what happened to Feingold, to be honest.

It just seemed like everything was aiming toward a total wipeout. But I thought Feingold had established himself as enough of a maverick and sort of a true son of Wisconsin politics that he would make it through.

ZALESKI: But it's not just that Feingold lost that's puzzling—but that he lost by over 100,000 votes.

GARVEY: That *was* a surprise because nobody knew what [Ron] Johnson was running on or what he stood for. I mean, it wasn't like people said, "Well, if we vote this way, we're going to get rid of Medicare and Medicaid and privatize Social Security and kill all the public employee unions." There was none of that. It was just that Feingold was too much of an insider.

So the Republicans promoted that Tea Party nonsense that if you've been in Washington more than ten minutes you're probably tainted. And I think a lot of people just got to the end of the game and froze and said, "I'm not going to participate. Let the Republicans have their chance, let's see what's going to happen here."

ZALESKI: So you think voters were just frustrated and shortsighted—that they decided, hey, Obama isn't the miracle worker we thought he was. So let's give the other guys another chance?

GARVEY: Yeah, I think so. It's the only explanation I have. I mean, nobody could have watched the single televised debate between Johnson and Feingold and concluded that Johnson was the superior intellect—or the better prepared or the more experienced. So what's the explanation that this sort of know-nothing is elected by defeating someone who's truly a national figure in Russ Feingold?

So my feeling has been that the destruction of the Democratic Party and its ability to respond to these situations began in Wisconsin with the creation of the legislative caucuses in the 1980s, where all the power of the party was shifted back into the hands of the incumbents, so that the face of the Democratic Party was the face of incumbency.

ZALESKI: So you reject the popular notion that voters were angry in this election, and by electing tough-talking guys like Walker and Johnson they were making a statement?

GARVEY: I didn't see that much anger. I mean, there may have been some. But I think that the Republicans' ground

game paid off. It was the fact, for instance, that the Feingold–
Johnson debates were a farce because they weren't carried by
very many TV stations. I mean, the one in Wausau, the second
one, supposedly was going to be carried by Channel 27 here in
Madison, but 27 decided not to carry it.

And when Feingold did appear in the debates with Johnson, it was no contest. I mean, Johnson seemed like a complete
Dodo bird compared to one of the brighter members of the
U.S. Senate. But the Republicans did beat the Democrats in
getting out the vote, knowing who to contact, who to appeal
to, and so forth.

So I don't see Walker's victory or Johnson's victory as a result of a great angst. I see it more as great organization.

ZALESKI: Why were so many average, middle-class voters
attracted to right-wing extremists like Walker and Johnson?

GARVEY: Well, I don't know, obviously. If I did, I'd be king,
I suppose. I didn't sense any great passion for Walker or Johnson. But there was no passion for [Walker's Democratic oppo-
nent] Tom Barrett, and really no passion for Feingold. I mean,
there was a commonly held belief that Russ was going to win,
that Democrats didn't have to worry about that race so much.

ZALESKI: What about the notion that voters were upset
about the unemployment situation in this country and the lack
of growth in the economy?

GARVEY: I think people were frustrated about those things—
and they still are. I mean, I think they're more frustrated now
about the tax breaks that are going to big corporations. What I
got from people prior to the midterms was kind of like, well,
Walker's probably bad, but he's not going to be any worse
than Tommy Thompson [Wisconsin's governor from 1987 to
2001].

That's what I think happened more than anything else.
Voters thought Barrett's not that exciting, the issues aren't that

big, Walker can't be that bad, so let's not get too excited about it.

ZALESKI: Still, you took some pretty hard shots at Thompson when you ran against him in 1998. How does Tommy compare to Walker?

GARVEY: Oh, Tommy's a moderate Democrat compared to this guy. I mean, this guy's dangerous. First off, Tommy, for whatever else you want to say about him, at least had some common sense and was fairly bright. This guy Walker has no common sense and is not very bright.

He doesn't know how to deal with the situation that's presented to him. He had this road map, sort of like the [Republican Representative] Paul Ryan road map: We're going to be quiet for the first month of November till January when we're sworn in. Then we're going to swoop down and say, "Ok, we're going to knock out the unions, we're going to knock out this, we're going to knock out that."

ZALESKI: Returning to Feingold, the general consensus— excluding conservatives—is that former Wisconsin Senator Gaylord Nelson was one of the finest senators in U.S. history. How does Feingold compare?

GARVEY: In terms of substance, I'd rank him right up there with Gaylord. But Russ never had the common touch of Gaylord Nelson. Gaylord could walk into a room and it would be ignited with his personality and his jokes and his ability to relate. Gaylord had it all.

Not only was he respected by his opponents, but they actually liked him—even Republicans who were opposed to his politics. Feingold had the intellectual package and certainly the respect of his colleagues, but people didn't have the same affection for Russ as they had for Gaylord.

ZALESKI: So if you were handing out grades, Nelson would get an A?

GARVEY: Without question.

ZALESKI: And Feingold?

GARVEY: A-minus. I mean, Russ is a helluva bright guy who took some courageous positions. I disagreed with him on always voting for the nominee from the Bush administration for the Supreme Court and so forth, but at least one understood where he was coming from; he wasn't selling out because of money. Nobody was giving him campaign contributions in order to be in favor of a Supreme Court nominee. He legitimately believed in what he was doing.

ZALESKI: Could Feingold have done anything different to prevent his defeat?

GARVEY: You know, a lot of us have spent a lot of time talking about that. I don't know. It seemed to me that what we worried about as the campaign got started was that there didn't seem to be much enthusiasm for Feingold's campaign from the outside.

It seemed like sort of an automated response, where Feingold was going to continue to go to seventy-two counties and have listening sessions but never a, "I'll give you a slap on the back and let's go have a beer." And by the time they figured out that you can have seventy-two listening sessions but if you add up the number of people who were there, it wouldn't be worth one TV spot, in terms of the size of the audience.

But it's easy to criticize other people's campaigns. It just seemed to me that the Feingold people weren't willing to warn people about just how dangerous this Johnson guy could be, and what could happen if the Republicans took over the U.S. Senate, and what was likely to occur.

2

SEEDS OF DEMISE

Still in a funk over the 2010 midterms, Garvey spent much of our second session expanding on his belief that anyone who was astounded by Scott Walker's ascent didn't understand the full picture. The Democratic Party, he maintained—both in Wisconsin and nationally—had planted the seeds of its own demise back in the 1980s when it began turning to well-heeled corporate interests to fund its campaigns and, in many cases, refused to even acknowledge that there were always strings attached to those contributions.

And now, he said with utter disgust, there was little to distinguish between the two parties. It was a point he'd made countless times in public appearances over the last two decades, and it infuriated him that few top-level Democrats would address the issue or even admit that big-money's top priorities didn't include boosting the quality of life for poor and middle-income Americans—one of the Democratic Party's base constituencies.

There was really only one prominent national politician, Senator Bernie Sanders, who wasn't afraid to state the obvious,

Garvey lamented as we settled into our chairs that morning. The Democratic Party had lost its soul. And he wasn't sure it could ever get it back.

●

ZALESKI: You said the destruction of the Democratic Party here in Wisconsin began with the forming of the legislative caucuses in the 1980s. Why was that so crucial?

GARVEY: Because that's when Democrat Chuck Chvala and Republican Scott Jensen and others became nonelected party leaders. I mean, they were elected as state legislators but there's no democracy within the Democratic Party anymore. And the same is true at the national level, where most politicians are millionaires who can't relate to middle-class or low-income Americans.

I mean, Jesus, I remember in 1985, when Nancy Pelosi first ran for chair of the Democratic National Committee. I was over in Milwaukee to give a talk to one of the Democratic Party units there. We were to meet in the back room of this bar on the near north side, and I got there a little early, so I thought I'd just have a beer at the bar and listen to the conversations. And most of the conversations were about how to properly dress a deer, how to gut it, and so on.

As that was going on, the Democratic National Committee was meeting in Puerto Rico. And the candidates for chair of the party were Nancy Pelosi, millionaire; Chuck Manatt, millionaire; and Paul Kirk, millionaire. I remember thinking, if you could bring those three people into this bar and get them into a discussion on how to gut a deer, it would be interesting to see their reactions.

Because they would have just gone, "Ewwww! Let's talk about something else and not even think about it." I mean, there's such a disconnect between the Democratic leadership and ordinary citizens these days that I don't think people have any sense anymore of what being a Democrat is about.

So when it came to Feingold in the midterms, I don't think voters felt any particular loyalty to him because he was a distant figure as far as they were concerned—so it wasn't their fight. I mean, when John Kennedy ran for president, working-class people felt it was *our* fight. Same thing with Bobby Kennedy and Hubert Humphrey, or Gaylord Nelson and Bob Kastenmeier. It was *our* fight.

ZALESKI: But the Kennedys were millionaires, and you had great admiration for them.

GARVEY: They *were* wealthy, but they were also involved. Bobby Kennedy would go into the black areas of Milwaukee, Chicago, or Newport, Indiana, and actually talk to people. In some ways, I think he was the last candidate for president who really felt he was part of that crowd out there. He could relate, there was a connection and a passion, and he had the ability to give people hope that they could rise out of poverty.

I mean, you can't go into Milwaukee on Juneteenth Day as a political candidate and walk down the street in some of the poor black neighborhoods without crying. You see hundreds of these beautiful black children, eight and nine years old, waving and having fun, and getting suckers and anything else people are throwing out the car windows, and you think, in two or three years, we'll have lost those kids. They're either going to go into the criminal justice system or they're going to get killed. And there's no sense among today's politicians that, hey, this crap has got to stop!

ZALESKI: But this is hardly a new development.

GARVEY: Right. When I was running for governor [in 1998], Barbara Lawton [Garvey's lieutenant governor running mate] and I had a meeting at a black church in Milwaukee for young black men who'd been incarcerated. And when we got to the

Q-and-A period, I called on this fellow and he said, "Mr. Garvey, I've never been habilitated, so how can I be rehabilitated?"

And it was, you know, one of those questions that stumps you, where you think, what do I say now? Finally I said, "I don't know what to tell you." And he said, "Well, nobody's ever told me how I'm supposed to live, or what I'm supposed to do, or where I need to go."

He said, "I'm an alcoholic but there are no treatment facilities around here that will take me. So what do I do? Who's going to help me?" It was sad, tragic—and I didn't have the answer.

ZALESKI: And your point is?

GARVEY: My point is, I think Bobby Kennedy and Gaylord Nelson and Lyndon Johnson, people like that, had some sense that these are our brothers and sisters—in a real way.

I mean, I don't think LBJ had to fake it. He really believed that we should get these people out of poverty. He certainly had a better grasp of the problem than a John Kerry or a Joe Lieberman or an Al Gore, the kind of stiffs who've come forward to represent the Democratic Party in the last decade or so. These guys don't see that the rich should pay anything. Or if they do see it, they're not saying it—because the rich contribute so much money to their campaigns they don't dare object to what the rich are doing.

So, no, the collapse of the Democrats didn't just happen at the midterms. It started happening shortly after Watergate, when we created the political action committees [PACs] and said, "Ok, this is somehow going to regulate the system."

Well, it was designed to fail because you could have 150 political action committees within the chemical industry, but the chemical workers could only have one. So the dice were loaded. And it just kept getting worse and worse. And the more the Democrats lost, the more they turned to the same corporate interests that were pouring money into Republican campaigns.

ZALESKI: Which you discovered when you ran against Senator Bob Kasten in 1986.

GARVEY: Yeah. I think Kasten raised about $3.4 million for his campaign, and we spent maybe $1.2 million, something like that. But given how close that race was, and given the resentment people felt toward Kasten for defeating maybe our greatest senator ever, Gaylord Nelson [in 1980], I should have won. But the amount of money they poured into their TV spots, which were designed by Roger Ailes, who was Kasten's campaign consultant, was just too much to overcome.

ZALESKI: And then Kasten ran that TV ad saying there was $750,000 missing from the NFLPA pension fund and that Ed Garvey didn't know where it went.

GARVEY: Right. We had just moved ahead of him in the polls when that ad came out. And we dropped I think fourteen points in two days. We ended up losing by about 2 percent. But it was abundantly clear that it was the TV spot that did it.

We sort of regained our momentum when we filed a libel action against him, and Ken Bowman and Gene Upshaw and other leaders of the NFL Players Association came out to Wisconsin to campaign for me, to show that there was no truth to this whole thing. But that was the Lee Atwater school of journalism—Ailes being Atwater's number one student—and it worked. And so they used that kind of negative stuff to really go after people from then on.

ZALESKI: Nonetheless, you believe, by and large, that the Democrats caused their own demise?

GARVEY: Absolutely. When you look at the Wisconsin Democratic Party or the slate of national candidates who've emerged in the last couple decades, you ask yourself, "Who selected these people?" I mean, in some respects the death knell in Wisconsin came when Herb Kohl announced that he was running for the U.S. Senate in 1988.

ZALESKI: Herb Kohl—that's where it started, in your view?

GARVEY: Oh yeah. The state Democratic Party met over in La Crosse that year, and Herb's people brought in a couple busloads of black kids from Milwaukee who were being paid the minimum wage to go to La Crosse to cheer for him. And there was a cheerleader who'd motion when they should applaud or yell or stand up or whatever.

And so Herb's giving this speech, which had about as much style and substance as something you'd expect from a third grader, and every minute or so you'd hear this loud "Yeaaaaah!!!!" And, of course, the rest of the Democratic Party in that room was practically all white. And that night I said to Betty, "When Herb wakes up tomorrow, he's going to ask himself, 'Whose idea was this? I've gotta get out of here.'"

Really, I thought he would drop out because it was so farcical. Well, instead of that, he put $5 million or $6 million into TV spots, and the spots were so effective that he won easily.

ZALESKI: Obviously, being a millionaire has worked in Kohl's favor every time he's been up for reelection, since he certainly doesn't generate much excitement—even among die-hard Democrats. But then, neither Feingold nor Barrett seemed to generate much excitement in this recent election either—nothing like we witnessed when Obama was elected in 2008.

GARVEY: Well, I used to talk to [the late Minnesota Senator] Paul Wellstone about this. He always said he was from the democratic wing of the Democratic Party. And he would say that if you make all the decisions in a small room somewhere and then tell people what they're going to do and what they're going to support and what they're going to fight for, it's pretty hard to get them excited about their task.

I mean, who really felt moved by this last election—in their gut? Intellectually, everybody said Feingold has to win. But I don't know a lot of people who said I'm going to quit my job and go work for Russ to get elected. And again, you take a politician like Herb Kohl. What's his mission? What does he stand for?

When he first ran in '88, he announced, "I am running for the Senate. I will develop my own platform, I will develop my own team, I will raise my own money, I will staff everything else. I don't need the party." And so, the party became irrelevant.

ZALESKI: But Kohl won.

GARVEY: That's right. And at that point everything about politics became more professionalized in a sense of people being hired to do what volunteers used to do. I mean, volunteers used to make the phone calls, knock on doors, and so forth. Now politicians pay people to make the calls, or you have these robo-calls. Or they pay people to go out on the street and knock on doors.

They pay people to answer the mail, to get involved in the process. So it's a different kind of commitment than the one I felt when I was out there handing out literature for [former Wisconsin Representative] Bob Kastenmeier. I mean, we believed in Bob. There was a reason to be out there.

The problem with most political candidates today is that they're selected by the incumbents from a pool of candidates who are mostly legislative aides or people who are acceptable to lobbyists and proposed by the wealthy. And these are not people who are likely to engender great passion.

So if you're a Democrat, blue-collar worker in 1992 and you see Bill Clinton fighting to see NAFTA [North American Free Trade Agreement] passed—and basically saying, "Forget about the jobs going out the window"—or as [third party presidential candidate] Ross Perot put it, "The whooshing sound you'll hear as businesses move to Mexico"—you say to yourself, "What the hell's going on here? How could a Democrat be leading that fight?" And then the fight is lost because NAFTA passes.

That's what's happening. And I think people in the factory know that. They understand that they're being used as cannon fodder.

ZALESKI: But isn't part of the problem the Democrats' inability to articulate why something like NAFTA will hurt blue-collar workers? I'd argue that most Americans still don't understand the downside to NAFTA.

GARVEY: Right. Because Democrats are afraid that if they do articulate them that the big business interests are going to cut them off financially. Former Senator Paul Simon [Democrat-Illinois] said it best. He'd talk about how he'd get finished with a day of campaigning and get back to the hotel, and there'd be little pink slips waiting for him to return phone calls.

He'd run through them, and if he saw the name of someone who'd given him $5,000 and he didn't recognize the other names—guess who he's going to call? He'd say, "Obviously I'm going to call the guy who gave me $5,000. Because I might get another $5,000." And that's the kind of stuff that turns most people off.

ZALESKI: And that was before the Supreme Court's Citizens United ruling opened the floodgates.

GARVEY: Oh, to be sure. When I was a kid, Gaylord and [Democratic Senator William] Proxmire had a wiener roast at one of the parks in Burlington. My parents went, and it was like $5 a person. And my dad told me later, "You know, they charged $5. And they couldn't have spent that much money on the food, because there wasn't much. But I guess they had to keep a little money for themselves and their campaigns, so it's ok."

And I laugh about that now, because if my father could see an invitation for some of these fund-raisers now—$1,000 for a cocktail party or a dinner—he'd say, "My God, how could a dinner possibly cost that much? I mean, what's going on here?"

But when people gave $5 so they could talk to Gaylord or [Democratic Representative] Henry Reuss or Kastenmeier, they gladly paid that amount because these were their guys! They wanted to hang out with them because they knew instinctively that these were the politicians who'd fight for them when they needed help. And that's all lost now. I mean, people don't have the sense that they can pick up the phone and call their congressman or their senator. They've lost the connection.

So the days of the $5 wiener roasts in the park have gone by the wayside. Today it's all about the money—big money. If you've got enough of it, you've got a chance. If you don't have the money, the press won't even cover you. I mean, you're irrelevant.

ZALESKI: Which you found out when you ran for governor in '98.

GARVEY: Exactly. I met with [Democrat] Tim John, from the Miller Brewing Company family, before he ran for governor last year [2010]. He came to me and said, "I want to run for governor, what do you think? I think I can win."

And I said, "Well, if you want to run, go ahead. But you're not going to win." He said, "Why not?" And I said, "Because you're not going to put $6 million or $7 million into it, and if you're not going to do that, you're not going to win."

He said, "Oh no, I think you're wrong. I can talk to the media." I told him, "The media doesn't give a shit. And more importantly, if you don't have $6 million or the ability to raise it, they won't cover you because they know you can't win—and if you can't win, why would they waste time covering you?"

Well, he was just shocked at my bluntness. And I told him, "You're not going to get anywhere with the Democrats themselves because they don't want to deal with you. They only want to deal with the people they've selected."

And, sorry to say, he found out I was right. [John was buried by Tom Barrett in the Democratic primary, getting just 9.5 percent of the vote.]

3

FIRESTORM ON THE SQUARE

In our first two sessions, Garvey had expressed hope that once working-class Americans in Wisconsin and elsewhere realized what Scott Walker and other far-right politicians were up to—that they were, in effect, devoted pawns for the Koch brothers, Wall Street, and other corporate schemers who were looking out for the upper 1 percent—they would come to their senses. But his words lacked conviction—as if he'd been delivering a pep talk but wasn't sure if he believed it himself.

But when we met again on another chilly but sunny morning in mid-March, his mood had been transformed almost overnight by the spontaneous firestorm that had ignited on the Capitol Square in downtown Madison. On March 12 more than 100,000 people—the largest turnout in a month-long series of highly vocal protests against Walker's anti-union campaign—had taken to the streets, and Garvey was almost giddy.

He was also dumbfounded. He couldn't believe that Walker, instead of being conciliatory and admitting he'd overreached, continued to—as Garvey put it—"pour gasoline on the fire" by chastising the protestors and refusing to budge from his hardline stance. And he was downright ecstatic that the extraordinary turnout had included not only large numbers of police, fire fighters, farmers, teachers, and students but the fourteen gallant Democratic senators—dubbed the "Fabulous 14"—who had temporarily fled the state rather than sit back and watch helplessly as the legislative-majority Republicans assailed the public employee unions.

This, Garvey was convinced, was a game-changer—the first visible signs that middle-class voters had awakened and recognized that they were being made scapegoats for the sour economy. And unless they fought back, their lives were about to undergo dramatic change and the financial pain inflicted on them would be felt for years.

This was real, it was palpable, and he couldn't wait to see what would happen next.

●

ZALESKI: While marveling at the size of the protest crowds here, liberal activist Michael Moore said, "The sleeping giant has been aroused" and suggested that there will be long-term implications. What's your take on what's occurring at the Capitol Square?

GARVEY: I think this is *the* turning point in Wisconsin politics. This is the most important period of time since—I don't know, maybe Joe McCarthy, maybe even before that. Because to get 100,000 people to do anything is incredible. I mean, I was talking to [state Democratic Senator] Fred Risser and various other people about the crowds up at the Capitol. During the Vietnam War era, where we shut down the state senate and so forth, if we got 3,000 people, that was an amazing turnout.

To see what we're seeing now—crowds of anywhere from 50,000 to 100,000—that's astonishing. And these people get it. They understand what the issue is. They understand that Michael Moore is right: it's not that Wisconsin's broke, as Scott Walker claims, or that the United States is broke. It's that there's too much power and too much money in too few hands. It's the distribution of the money, not the fact that we're broke.

I mean, how the hell can we be broke? If you're broke you don't give $100 million in tax breaks to corporations, like Walker just did. You say, "This is a time for all of us to sacrifice." But the Republican line is consistent whether it's [Governor Chris] Christie in New Jersey, [Governor John] Kasich in Ohio, [Governor Mitch] Daniels in Indiana, or Walker in Wisconsin. This is a well-connected plan by the Tea Party, funded by the billionaire Koch brothers and others, to really define this plutocracy that we're now living with.

So I think what's happening in Madison is an extraordinarily important moment. If the "Fabulous 14" survive, and we're able to recall some of those Republican senators this summer, it will go down in history as the time when Wisconsin once again turned to its progressive past to become a state with a future.

ZALESKI: You're encouraged by the "Wisconsin 14's" willingness to leave Wisconsin to state their case?

GARVEY: Oh, absolutely. And the fact that they're fourteen individual personalities, and fourteen people who have their own lives to lead, and fourteen people who have to trust one another . . . I think they've just been magnificent.

ZALESKI: Did their actions surprise you?

GARVEY: Yeah. I mean, I don't want to say I expected them to fold, but any time you get fourteen people under that much pressure—it's sort of like when union people say you should have work slowdowns as opposed to a strike. The problem with work slowdowns is that the pressure is all on the individual. So if over at station ten the guy is committed to the slowdown, management knows that he's slowed down—and they can say, "If you don't get back to your normal speed you're fired." The idea of collective action is that the individual never faces that individual pressure. You have the group that takes on the pressure.

But with the "Wisconsin 14," all the pressure was on these fourteen people. So it's a helluva lot more difficult to deal from that card game than it is to get a couple busloads of people to march around the Capitol Square. So, yeah, I'm really impressed with the fact that leadership has developed within that group. They've been very articulate in expressing their position, and they've been steadfast in saying, "We're not going to sell out, we're not going to give up."

ZALESKI: Many people—and not just those protesting at the Capitol—seem shocked by Walker's hubris. It's similar to the attitude of Florida's new Republican governor, Rick Scott, another Tea Party favorite, who, like Walker, turned down federal money for high-speed rail in his state. What do you make of that?

GARVEY: Well, I think it's part of their training. I mean, the Republican candidates *are* trained these days. It's like if you watch any of these conservative talk shows. Ann Coulter, for instance, knows how to talk right through you, so that whoever is sitting opposite her can never get in a word edgewise; [Bill] O'Reilly same thing. They just force their way past you and there's nothing you can do about it.

I think somebody like Walker, he's surrounded by the Bradley Foundation [a private, conservative grant making organization in Milwaukee] and the Koch brothers—the experts in rhetoric and in organization. They give him a sense of confidence that he can pull it off, and it's almost as if he's invincible. They obviously told him that in his inaugural address he needed to say, "Here's the problem, we're broke. And we need extraordinary measures to deal with the fact that we're broke—and here they are. And you've got to live with these measures because otherwise we're going to go under."

And they assumed people would agree with that and that there wouldn't be the pushback that there was. They just figured they could push it right on through, and that when people woke up and found out the unions were busted, that local governments were screwed, school class sizes were doubled, research was stopped, jobs were leaving Wisconsin, and so forth . . . at that point they'd say, "Well, we've taken these much-needed corrective steps, but don't worry too much because now all these corporations from across the country are going to want to move here."

And I'm thinking, let me get this right. You're the CEO of a big corporation and you're watching all this and now you're saying, "Why don't we just relocate to Wisconsin, because Wisconsin's not going to have more money for tourism this year? Their schools will be hurting, the university is going to be spun off to the private sector, and there are going to be demonstrations all over the place, so why don't we go to Wisconsin?"

That really makes a helluva lot of sense. I mean, it's all so ridiculous.

ZALESKI: According to a recent piece in *The Progressive* magazine, Walker committed to Jesus at age thirteen, and God has told him what to do regarding every important decision he's made—such as whom to marry and whether to run for governor.

GARVEY: And I talked to God the other day, and he said, "Sorry, I've got to put you on hold because Scott Walker is calling."

Yeah, the religious influence with some of these politicians today. . . . You know, I grew up in an interesting family. My mom was Protestant and my dad was Catholic. She hated the Catholic Church, and he hated the clergy. But one time I was having an argument in high school with friends in our living room, and I was telling them that Martin Luther was wrong, that he should have stayed within the church. And my friend was arguing in favor of Martin Luther, and he got up and left. And my dad, who was sitting in the TV room, says, "Eddie, come in here."

So I went into the TV room, and he said, "Neither one of you knows what you're talking about. And you're making a fool of yourself. But I'm going to tell you something—your friend's religious views are none of your business. And your religious views are none of his business. And there will be no more discussions in this house about religion." He said, "You want to argue about religion, go someplace else, but not in this house."

And my parents, from day one, said, "One of the great things about this country is we're free from religious rulers. That's why your grandparents came to this country—to escape the English, but also to escape the domination of the church." So to me, the idea of Scott Walker talking to God—he ought to be examined by a psychiatrist, I would think, at a minimum. Jesus, "I'm talking to God?" Whoa.

ZALESKI: Lee Dreyfus [the charismatic Republican and former University of Wisconsin–Stevens Point chancellor who served as Wisconsin's governor from 1979 to 1983] used to say, "I'm always wary of somebody who claims they know what God is thinking."

GARVEY: Which brings to mind another story. The nuns at my school would get pretty excited because I had a Protestant mother. So one day my sixth-grade nun pulled me aside and said, "We want you to go home and try to convince your mother to join the Catholic Church so she can go to heaven." So I'm at dinner that night and I said, "Mother, I'd like you to become a Catholic." And my dad said, "Who asked you?" I said, "Sister Marianne." He said, "Well, you tell her to keep her damn nose out of our business, and we'll keep our nose out of her business."

And I said, "But don't you think mother wants to go to heaven with us?" He looked at me and said, "What's wrong with you?" Then he asked me, "Do you think your grandfather's going to go to heaven?" I said, "Of course. He's a doctor up in Oshkosh, just a wonderful guy." And my dad says, "So why would he go to heaven and not your mother?" And that was sort of the end of that.

ZALESKI: Returning to the protest rallies, you think this is just the beginning?

GARVEY: Oh yeah. This is something you couldn't manufacture. If you said, "Look, what we want is to get 100,000 people up on the Capitol Square, marching and being willing to go to jail if necessary on behalf of public finance campaigns or whatever. . . ." No way! You'd be lucky to get a carload of people to go up there. This guy Walker has set off an explosion that no one can fully explain—and he keeps throwing kerosene on the flames. And every time you think this thing might be slowing down, whoosh! Up it goes again.

ZALESKI: So as demoralizing as his victory over Barrett was, you're now encouraged?

GARVEY: Oh, I'm very encouraged. Yeah. I think it's a very exciting moment.

ZALESKI: Do you think the outrage displayed here will carry over to the 2012 elections?

GARVEY: Oh, I don't have any doubt about that.

ZALESKI: Many progressives—not just here, but across the

country—have expressed bafflement and exasperation that Obama hasn't been here for the protests, or, at the very least, Joe Biden or someone else from his administration.

There have been news reports that Obama's staffers, namely Chief of Staff William Daley and Senior Adviser David Plouffe, have advised him not to come. Should he have ignored them and come anyway?

GARVEY: Absolutely he should have been here. If the president can't stand behind working people when their existence is at stake, what is a Democrat? And where is the Democratic Party, for that matter? Where are the Al Gores and the John Kerrys? These guys don't think twice about jumping on a plane and flying to Libya or Iraq or Afghanistan. And they won't come to Madison?

I mean, think about it. There've been almost no national figures who've come to Madison to support the workers here. Michael Moore is one, but he's a fringer, as I am. But where are these leaders? Where's Howard Dean, the former chair of the Democratic National Committee?

ZALESKI: How do you explain it?

GARVEY: That they think they can then play it down the middle. They rationalize that there will be voices on the left and voices on the right, so we'll play it down the middle so that independents will vote for us because we're not left or right. I think it's just a cold, calculated decision that staying away is good for Obama.

ZALESKI: So, it's just another example of the Democratic Party having lost its way?

GARVEY: Oh yeah. The Democratic Party has just been missing in action for some time now. In fact, I just read that Lawrence O'Donnell at the White House was very upset with the Democratic National Committee for using some Obama organizers to support the workers here. Well, what the hell.

How can that be? And we haven't even had that many promi-nent Wisconsin Democrats involved in these protests either. I mean, I haven't seen [former Democratic governor] Tony Earl. I haven't seen Herb Kohl.

ZALESKI: Why would some state Democratic leaders not show up?

GARVEY: Same thing. When Herb decided to run for U.S. Senate, he had the money to do it, and he created his own pro-gram. He's an independent entity. He's not a Democrat in the sense that Dave Obey is a Democrat or that Ed Garvey is a Democrat. It's not based on solidarity forever, it's more based on the enjoyment of the office and doing some good for people. But it's a far cry from what I think is needed.

ZALESKI: Ed Schultz and other liberal pundits have said in recent days that ignoring what's been occurring in Madison was a huge miscalculation by the Obama administration—and that it could end up haunting Obama in 2012. Do you agree?

GARVEY: Yeah, I think so. Why wouldn't you want to stand with the workers? It's incredible. But, then again, why would you choose someone like Bill Daley as your chief of staff? I mean, just look at his ties to the investment world and so forth. You knew immediately that his appointment wasn't going to be good news for progressives. So the fact that Obama has held back and pretended that nothing important was taking place here . . . I think Ed Schultz nailed it better than anybody else when he asked on his show, "Mr. President, where are you? What are you doing?"

I wrote basically the same thing on my blog [on fightingbob .com] the other day. I said, "Mr. President, when you were in trouble while running for president, you came to Madison for a tremendous rally of students and faculty and union mem-bers and other working-class people who believed in your candidacy. So where are you now when we need you? And if you continue to turn your back, remember that when you run for reelection and want to return here in 2012—because how many of us do you think are going to show up? You might want to think about going to some other city."

So, in answer to your question, I do think Obama's made a huge miscalculation in not coming here because I think this is a watershed moment for the Democratic Party. I don't know if it means a third party or what, but the loyalty factor sure has eroded. Oh my goodness, what a missed opportunity.

ZALESKI: Judging from Walker's victory and those of other conservative Republicans in the midterms, it appears that a fairly large percentage of Americans do, in fact, disdain and mistrust unions. Why do you think that is?

GARVEY: I don't think they do, to be honest. I think you've got a kept media that keeps saying that. It's kind of like when I was running the NFL Players Association, when I kept hearing from people like Bob Wolf [former sports columnist for the old *Milwaukee Journal*] and other writers around the country that the fans all supported the owners.

Then Lou Harris did a poll, and it turned out the fans supported the players by about two to one. And, of course, the sports columnists—Dave Anderson of the *New York Times* was another one who railed against the players union—couldn't believe it. I don't think Dave Anderson has recovered to this day. They just couldn't figure out how the fans could possibly support those ingrates called athletes. I mean, for God's sake, there must be something wrong!

ZALESKI: A recent *USA Today* poll showed that 61 percent of Americans strongly oppose laws taking away the collective bargaining rights of public employee unions. But those who *are* anti-union seem to despise everything they stand for. How do you account for it?

GARVEY: Well, part of it is that the union-busting efforts by those on the far right have been pretty successful—wherever they can zero in on a particular industry or business and try to destroy the union, they do it, using the same techniques they use in a political campaign. They talk about how much money the union officials are earning, about how much it cost, and they come up with all this garbage about being forced to join a union. They paint this picture of a gulag where everybody's forced to march lockstep behind the union leadership, which is of course absolute nonsense.

And the labor laws in this country haven't been enforced for thirty years—and when they are enforced, there are never any penalties that adequately punish those scofflaws who violate the law. So if you own a company and are trying to stop a union from organizing in your plant, you fire the union leaders. What happens? Well, four or five years down the road there might be an unfair labor charge where the company is found guilty—which usually means reinstatement, maybe with back pay.

By now, however, the worker's gone or he's taken another job or he's died or is incapacitated or whatever. So the incentive for companies is to fire the union leadership so that you can get rid of the union rather than sit down and bargain.

ZALESKI: Whatever the case, there's no denying that there's a fair amount of anti-union sentiment among middle- and low-income people, particularly in rural areas—the kind of people who helped elect Scott Walker. They seem to resent that union members, through tough bargaining, earn decent paychecks and have good benefits. Is a lot of it jealousy—because their own jobs don't provide similar benefits and security?

GARVEY: I think so, to some extent. But I think what's happening right now with this battle in Wisconsin is that people are beginning to understand that the far right first succeeded in killing private-sector pensions, and now they're going after public pensions as well—teachers' pensions, for instance. So I think workers more and more are beginning to understand that, as Cesar Chavez said, "Hang together or hang separately."

ZALESKI: Those who oppose unions claim they've become too powerful.

GARVEY: Yeah, that's the cliché. They'd like you to believe that. But where's the power? I mean, for God's sake . . .

ZALESKI: One complaint is that companies with strong unions often can't make any work-environment changes unless they're approved by the union first.

GARVEY: Yeah, you hear that—which is crazy. The whole concept of collective bargaining is that you eliminate government intervention and you have democracy within the plant or the organization—and the concept is that those who make the rules are part of that entity. So there's a common stake in making sure the company is doing well, that they are making quality Harley-Davidson motorcycles, for instance, and are selling them at a reasonable price. I mean, both sides have the incentive to work together and not separately.

So the idea that the unions are standing in the way of progress—where? How about the UAW's [United Auto Workers] concessions that helped Chrysler and General Motors survive during the financial meltdown? As [the late University of Wisconsin law professor] Nate Feinsinger used to say, it's shop-floor democracy that makes America unique. Well, it's no longer unique, but it's what convinces people on both sides to work together.

ZALESKI: Certainly someone like Obama understands how it works. So you really do have to question what he and his chief advisors were thinking when they saw the tens of thousands of protestors at the Capitol—and did nothing. It's especially baffling considering the immense lift Obama got from his two rallies on the UW–Madison campus—one during his campaign in 2008 and the other just last year [2010], when thirty thousand people showed up.

GARVEY: Exactly. Which just proves that his absence at the recent protests here was a calculated move. He didn't go to Ohio either—or New Jersey or Indiana. Which is too bad because this is really a phenomenal movement. So for Obama to just sit it out is bizarre.

Rose Ann DeMoro [executive director of National Nurses United, the nation's largest nurses' union], said recently she'll buy the president a pair of comfortable shoes if he promises to live up to his campaign pledge—but apparently even that doesn't seem to bother him. [In a 2007 speech, Obama had said, "If American workers are being denied the right to organize and collectively bargain when I'm in the White House, I'll put on a comfortable pair of shoes myself. I'll walk that picket line with you as President of the United States of America, because workers deserve to know that somebody is standing in their corner."]

ZALESKI: It is hard to believe he'd go back on his word.

GARVEY: Yeah, it does. Because he's never going to have a better opportunity than this. I mean, if he came here and walked this line, he could duck practically all the other issues where liberals disagree with him. Everybody who supports working-class Americans would give him a pass! Now they're not going to give him a pass on anything.

ZALESKI: Some might conclude that Obama's refusal to come here is proof that it's hopeless—that Wall Street, the bankers, and corporate America do own the politicians, and nobody's about to cross them.

GARVEY: It's *not* hopeless! And I'll tell you when I really started to feel excited—when Ed Sadlowski, who ran for

On February 15, 2011, tens of thousands of people storm Madison's Capitol Square to protest newly elected governor Scott Walker's anti-union agenda. (*State Journal* archives)

president of the steelworkers union years ago, came to Madison [for the protests], and I got together with him and his son, Ed Jr., who used to work for Madison Teachers Inc. and is a good friend of mine.

I said, "Let's go up at the top of the Concourse Hotel and look down at the crowd, just to get some gauge of how big it is." So we did—and it was just enormous! I don't know if it was 100,000 or 120,000. Whatever it was, it was so much bigger than anything we'd ever seen in this country—that I'd seen anyway. At the peak of the anti–Vietnam War effort we never got a crowd that big. At least, I don't recall seeing one that big.

And when you saw these people with their homemade signs, identifying the real issues—like the maldistribution of income—and that they're concerned about health care, they're concerned about public education, they want to fight for their police officers and teachers and fire fighters and their nurses and so on—well, it gives you hope that Americans may finally be awakening to the fact that they've been had!

So I started getting pretty excited, thinking, wow, if we can maintain this momentum, defeat [incumbent conservative justice] David Prosser in the April 5 Supreme Court election, and recall three or four of those Republican state senators, we may be returning to the days of La Follette—when they kicked the corporations out of politics and turned the spoils system into the civil service system. Where you could get rid of the utility-dominated public service system and actually have a public-dominated public service commission. So I had a renewed faith that if people really give a damn, they can make the changes we need. I mean, the biggest enemy we've had for years is that cynical feeling that there's nothing you can do, so why do it? If you can't get over that, you just can't win.

ZALESKI: So you truly believe this is a watershed moment—a moment that could trigger a rebirth of the progressive movement that Fighting Bob ignited more than a century ago?

GARVEY: I think it is. And if we lose this momentum, I don't know if we'll ever get it back. But I do think that there has to be some fear on the side of the Republicans at this point—not only the ones in office, but the Koch brothers and the others on the far right. They *never* anticipated that 100,000 people would show up to protest what Walker and the other Republicans here have done—that you'd have small farmers arm in arm with automakers, and automakers arm in arm with teachers; that you'd have the public sector understanding the private sector, and the private sector understanding the public sector. And it's happened! And I think it's probably scaring the hell out of the zealots on the far right.

ZALESKI: And the biggest worry for leaders of this movement is that the masses who showed up for the protests will return to their cozy little worlds and never be heard from again. It's a very real possibility.

GARVEY: Right, that's our concern. And the concern of the Koch brothers and people like Scott Walker is that the protestors stay active and get even angrier and more militant. I mean, the protestors who marched around the Capitol were a very polite crowd. If they really get angry at what's happening, the Republicans aren't sure how it will end up. I mean, look at what's happened in Tunisia and Egypt.

It seems farfetched, and I'm loath to make those comparisons for the obvious reason, but there was a demand made by young people [in those countries] that they have freedom—the freedom meaning jobs and economic development and the opportunity to live a decent life. And if you can't get jobs for people who are unemployed, the American people are not just going to take this lightly. It's not going to be a fun place to be.

ZALESKI: The key, it seems to me, is to find a way to reach students and other young people who are facing a bleak economic future—to keep them engaged and fired up, just like they were for Obama in 2008.

GARVEY: I agree. But, unfortunately, he sent them back to their world. That's the part that's most disturbing. It's going to be hard to get young people or progressive ideologues of any age to get involved again because Obama's let them down on virtually every issue.

4

EXTREMISTS TAKE CONTROL

I suspected Ed would be in a foul mood when we got together for our next session—and I was right. A week earlier, a
long-shot progressive candidate named Joanne Kloppenburg
had nearly toppled conservative incumbent David Prosser in
one of the wildest and most contentious Supreme Court elections in state history.

In fact, Kloppenburg had actually been declared the victor
until the day after the election when Kathy Nickolaus, the
clerk in conservative Waukesha County—who had worked for
Prosser in the Capitol a decade earlier—claimed that the results from the city of Brookfield weren't reported to the Associated Press on election night because of "human error." Thus,
Prosser had actually won by 7,500 votes.

Garvey smelled a rat. What's more, he was deeply concerned that the size of the protest crowds at the Capitol was
beginning to wane. (They all but stopped in June when Wisconsin Act 10—Walker's budget repair bill—was upheld by
the State Supreme Court.)

Still, he was quick to note that there was a growing fear nationwide—even among many moderates—that right-wing extremists had hijacked the Republican Party. So in this session we talked about whether there was any plausible explanation for what was happening—and whether there was anything progressives could do to counteract the alarming shift that threatened to disrupt their daily lives.

●

ZALESKI: We've talked about how an endless torrent of special-interest money has poisoned our political system over the last three decades. But that's hardly the only obstacle reform-minded, liberal candidates face. A week after the midterms, a Gallup poll pretty much confirmed what many on the left suspected: 42 percent of Americans consider themselves conservative, 35 percent are moderate, and just 20 percent are liberal.

How do you account for that? Some maintain it's because Republicans have succeeded in attracting middle-class voters by emphasizing hot-button issues like abortion, gay marriage, and gun control.

GARVEY: Well, first of all, I have no idea what questions the Gallup people asked. But let's assume it's an accurate poll. Well, if you asked me to define what being a liberal is, I'd have trouble answering that. Or what is a Democrat? I'd have trouble with that too.

And if I have trouble articulating what it means to be a Democrat today—and I've spent a big part of my adult life running for office or trying to frame the issues—how about everybody else?

I mean, when John Kennedy established the Peace Corps, was that a liberal program? Is Social Security a liberal program? The labels have lost all meaning because the consultants now say to the candidates, "Here's how you have to frame this issue so you can get all left-handed golfers who have a six handicap or less to support it. You can't say you're pro women's rights and pro-gun control. You've got to be evasive so you can attract a larger following."

ZALESKI: One of the biggest frustrations among progressives is that Republicans have somehow succeeded in turning liberal into a dirty word, especially for many working-class people—and they end up voting against their own economic interests. Do you agree with that assessment?

GARVEY: Pretty much. I mean, after [Pulitzer Prize–winning author] Theodore White wrote his *The Making of the President* books, I had the privilege of being at a meeting in New York where he spoke.

And he essentially said that Madison Avenue is so good that they get people to pay more money for, say, Bayer aspirin than for regular aspirin because they convince people it's better because it has the Bayer name on it. And he said if they can do that, and they can aim their advertising campaigns at young black men and young black women and young Hispanic voters or whatever, they have such an enormous advantage because they're able to frame the issues in such a way that they get the majority of people on your side.

So I see what's happened as the influence of Madison Avenue more than anything else—where the worker who's struggling to keep his or her nose above the water line economically sees the thirty-second Republican TV spots that suggest these Democrats or these liberals are against you—that they're going to take more money out of your pockets. And if there's no adequate response from Democrats, these struggling workers say, "Well, son of a bitch, why would I support them? They're going to take money out of my pocket!"

So I think Madison Avenue and the Republicans have captured the day because they've captured the rhetoric. They've framed the issues and the debate, and they select the candidates to run on the basis of the programs they've developed.

ZALESKI: So to a large extent, it's an inability of the Democrats to counteract these messages?

GARVEY: It's the Democrats not stepping forward and saying, "Here's what it means to be a Democrat." So today, instead of Bobby Kennedy or Bob Kastenmeier, you get the kind of Blue Dog Democrats, who are saying, "It's more important to kowtow to the interests of the rich, so we can get the money."

The argument that drives me the craziest is, "Look, if I don't raise the money I can't get into position to do the good that you want to have done." But what happens, of course, is— [former Wisconsin governor] Jim Doyle is a perfect example. When he first ran in 2002, he promised to reform campaign finance. That was his number one issue. Then he gets elected governor and suddenly people are throwing money at him— Jesus, he's like one of those dancers from those Al Capone movies, where people are stuffing $100 bills in their bras. Although I must say it's a little hard for me to imagine Jim Doyle in that position.

But, as I just mentioned, Democrats like Jim Doyle defend their actions by saying, "Unless we raise the money, we can't get elected. And if we can't get elected we can't implement our programs." What they fail to come to grips with is, if they lose their soul in the panic to get the money, they're going screw it up anyway. And they're not going to use the money in the people's best interests because they've been compromised.

ZALESKI: Doyle, it turned out, was never actually serious about campaign finance reform. Why do you think that was?

GARVEY: Hell, why should he? He could raise a ton of money from special interests. And so more and more Democrats are sending the message out to people—"Look, we're just part of the Money Party. They've got a branch over there called Republicans, and we've got the Democrats over here. And there's no real difference between the two of us."

And, frankly, there's an element of truth here. If you don't have money, then you probably can't win. And it becomes a self-fulfilling prophecy because the media says, "Well, you don't have the money, you can't win, therefore you're not going to win"—and they don't win! And the media says, "We were right."

ZALESKI: Many would argue that the Democrats aren't solely to blame for their demise. They believe a big reason for the Dems' inability to connect with voters is because many Americans are being manipulated by Fox News, right-wing talk radio, and conservative cable TV pundits—have been for years. How else does one explain that just a few weeks before the 2004 presidential election, a poll showed that 62 percent of Americans still thought Saddam Hussein was involved in 9/11?

GARVEY: [Liberal pundits] Bill Moyers and Kevin Phillips had a discussion a couple years ago in which they talked about class warfare. And Moyers said, "The rich declared class warfare in 1984, and they have won." And Phillips said, "You're right—because the fact is, big money now controls both parties."

He said, "It's no disgrace that it controls the Republican Party—that's why you have a Republican Party. It's for the wealthy. The sin is that it's also taken over the Democratic Party." And if you can't make distinctions between the parties, then people slip off into things like right to life or gun control.

Or whether gays should be able to walk down the street during daylight—whatever the issue.

So I think it's the big money interests who've figured out how you can take a democracy and turn it into a plutocracy. It's not parents and it's not the schools and it's not the press. It's the special interests who are pouring money into these campaigns so that they can buy the message they want out there.

ZALESKI: But don't you think the Republicans' ability to do that—to manipulate voters—suggests a failing of our educational system as well?

GARVEY: Well, sure it does. We understood more about civics when I was in high school than any of these kids do today—or seem to. But I think kids today are probably less susceptible to the BS than adults are. Because through the Internet and so on, they've been able to question some of the verities that we hold dear.

So I think if young people get a chance to run for office, they'll be better than we were. Unfortunately, they don't have a chance. They're not going to win—because of the money.

ZALESKI: But how do you explain that, even today, many Americans still believe Saddam was directly involved in 9/11?

GARVEY: Well, you have to remember that George Bush and the vice president and the secretary of defense all said, "Hey, Saddam has weapons of mass destruction"—and most people want to believe their government. And they want to believe that the president isn't going to lie to them. So if the president says, "Saddam is behind this," I think the national instinct is, "Well, he knows more than we know. He's gets his daily briefings, he knows what's going on. So it must be true."

It's hard for people to accept the idea that the president is totally corrupted by the money that Halliburton and others are going to make from the war effort itself—probably because they project their own values into the candidates and they don't think about a young man or a young woman going off to war in Afghanistan.

I mean, I've been seeing these people in the airports the last couple weeks. I want to go up to them and say, "I'm sorry. I mean, Christ, why are we putting you in harm's way?" Most people look at that war right now and say, "They shouldn't be in harm's way, they shouldn't be there." But if the president says this is absolutely essential to the long-term peace, you've got to go along with it.

ZALESKI: And unfortunately, as we've talked about, there really doesn't seem to be much difference between Democrats and Republicans today. Certainly not like the old days.

GARVEY: Yeah, it's very sad. The Wisconsin Democratic Party has a leadership training program of sorts, and they meet up at Devil's Lake. It's mostly for high school and college kids—the party's trying to introduce them into the political mainstream. Which is good.

About eight years ago, [then a state Democratic Representative] Mark Pocan called me and said, "Something came up and Russ Feingold can't give the speech tomorrow. Can you do it?" And I said, "Yes, I'm available, but you'll get kicked out of the party if you invite me to talk to these folks." He laughed and said, "Let's have some fun with it."

So I drove over to Devil's Lake and walked into the meeting. And I'll tell you, I had no trouble getting to the coffee machine because the people who were there parted like Moses and the Red Sea. Nobody wanted to have anything to do with me.

ZALESKI: Which, I suspect, you're used to by now?

GARVEY: Of course. But I walk in and there's a room full of bright, young, mostly white kids who were interested in politics. I'd heard that their speaker the day before told them how

to finesse issues so they wouldn't get caught on the pro-choice
or pro-life question, or vouchers vs. non-vouchers. In other
words, they were told how to slide down the middle.

So I looked at this group and said, "Look, folks, if you're
here because you want somebody to call you governor, assemblyman, senator, or president, you're in the wrong room. Go
join the Republicans. They have more money, they have a better
plan, they serve much better food—and their wine is superb!
And if that's why you're in politics, you might as well enjoy
yourself.

"If, on the other hand, you're here because you couldn't
look a young black couple in the face and say, 'Your child
can't get treated for this illness because you don't have health
insurance'—and you're mad as hell because of that, you're in
the right room! Because we won't tolerate this kind of crap."

So I get a nice ovation from the crowd, and as I'm leaving,
the husband of a top Democratic Party official says to me,
"Well, I think they should have heard something like that.
That was probably ok." And I'm thinking, you son of a bitch. I
mean, what are we raising? Why did I get involved in politics?
I got involved because I was inspired by Eleanor Roosevelt
and by Gaylord and by Martin Luther King and on and on.

The message that was being conveyed to these young people
who wanted to get into politics was, "Don't take strong stands
on issues because you'll alienate some people—and you might
alienate the funders. And if you alienate the funders, well,
screw it, you're done anyway."

So did the midterms just happen? I don't think so. I think
they happened when the seeds were sown back in the seventies
and eighties, and we're just seeing the effects of that today.

5

KID FROM BURLINGTON

Even many of his detractors would concede that one of Garvey's great charms—which served as a useful counterbalance to his hair-trigger temper—was his self-deprecating wit. If you spoke to him at length, you could expect that every so often he'd crack a wry smile and refer to himself as "some kid from Burlington." As in, "but then, what would some kid from Burlington, Wisconsin, know about that?" Fully aware, of course, that the kid from Burlington had, by his twenties, evolved into an intellectual warrior who would go on to record a long list of noteworthy triumphs.

Almost invariably, whenever I interviewed Ed over the years about a particular issue or event, we'd end up reminiscing about his days as executive director of the NFLPA—which, he'd quickly note, was one heckuva long way from Burlington, Wisconsin. And then, without fail, he'd point out—though never in much detail—that he was also deeply involved in the early days of the civil rights movement.

The reason this fascinated me, I'm sure, is because I—like Garvey—grew up in a predominantly white community (Bay

View, on Milwaukee's blue-collar south side) in the 1950s and '60s. And outside of my older sister LeeAnne, I knew of no one in my neighborhood who expressed empathy over what blacks in the South were experiencing at the hands of hate-spewing white racists in the turbulent early sixties.

"Change will come, they need to be patient," was a common refrain. But I do remember being shocked in 1964, my junior year at Milwaukee Bay View High, when George Wallace, the rabble-rousing, race-baiting governor of Alabama, got 34 percent of the vote while finishing second in the Wisconsin Democratic presidential primary. It was my first realization that the state I loved was far more racist than I ever thought possible—and it disturbed me profoundly.

So when Ed and I met for our next interview on another raw, gray morning, I was eager to explore this part of his life—how a kid from lily-white Burlington in the fifties began his long, slow transformation into one of the most outspoken and dynamic liberal activists in Wisconsin's history.

●

ZALESKI: We've talked about the need to get young people involved in the progressive movement—the ones largely responsible for the election of Barack Obama. I'm curious about your own roots—how, for example, does a kid from a small farm town in southeastern Wisconsin become a flaming liberal?

GARVEY: Yeah, it's hard to be a liberal growing up in Burlington, which had about four thousand people in those days—not much smaller than it is today. My dad had his own business, Garvey Pharmacy, and I had two older sisters [Gail and Jean]—I was the picked-on baby in the family. We had a wonderful home.

My mother was a home-economics teacher in Omro [in north-central Wisconsin] when she met my dad, but in

Ed with his father, Edward C. Garvey, in the backyard of their Burlington home. The elder Garvey owned and operated Garvey Pharmacy. (Garvey family photo)

Burlington, you couldn't teach if you were a married woman at that time. That's actually true. [Laughs.]

I started working in my dad's drug store when I was in second grade, dusting off bottles, marking newspapers, that sort of thing. On Sunday mornings, I'd go to 6:00 mass, then rush down and open the store. Imagine today letting a young kid open a store at 8 in the morning. . . . I mean, it would never happen. But in those days it was very safe and everybody felt

Young Ed and his fa-
vorite pet, "Lambie."
(Garvey family photo)

comfortable. My dad would go to 7:30 mass and then he'd get to the store about 8:30.

ZALESKI: Any memories stand out?

GARVEY: Sure. One that stands out was the day my sister brought some kids from Milwaukee's inner city to visit. They played outside and, after lunch, none of the neighbor kids was allowed to come back out and play. I never saw a black person in the drug store in all the years I worked there. I don't think I ever saw a black person in Burlington, period—they just didn't come into town.

You'd see Negroes fishing off the railroad bridges, which was common in a lot of small towns. But that was sort of the extent of integration in the 1940s and '50s.

Throughout his life, Ed was a standout golfer. At fourteen, he won the State Youth Amateur Championship. He later captained the University of Wisconsin golf team. (Garvey family photo)

ZALESKI: What was your childhood like? Did you ever get into trouble?

GARVEY: That's always a hard question to answer. Besides working in my dad's store, I played golf at Brown's Lake golf course and was captain of my high school team, went to school dances, whatever. I wasn't a great athlete, but I was a good golfer and was lucky enough to win the State Youth Amateur Championship when I was fourteen.

I always got along well with just about everybody. I was elected mayor of the school, so I was the one dealing with the administration over issues like student court or whether the principal should have authority over the students or whether the students should have authority over themselves.

I was a B student probably. My sisters were always A students, valedictorians. I never aspired to be quite that good. I

Ed was a B student at Burlington High School but didn't get serious about scholastics until he attended the University of Wisconsin in the late 1950s. (Garvey family photo)

got along fine, didn't have too many problems in high school, never got into serious trouble. We'd steal watermelons and pumpkins from the farmers and stuff like that, and you'd get rock salt shot at you from the porch but that was about it. Tipped over a few outhouses on Halloween.

ZALESKI: And your first liberal heroes?

GARVEY: Well, the first politician I ever met was Robert Taft [conservative Republican senator from Ohio], strangely enough. My mother took me to this breakfast in Burlington to meet Taft, who was running against [Dwight] Eisenhower for the Republican nomination in 1952. And so I met him, and that sort of interested me in terms of what politics was about.

I was about 12. Then I started paying attention to Senator Adlai Stevenson of Illinois, the Democratic nominee for president in 1952 and '56. He was probably the first national figure that sort of grabbed my attention.

ZALESKI: What did your parents think of that?

GARVEY: Well, my dad had been a good Democrat in Prairie du Chien, where he was raised. But he got so upset with the negative campaigning against [Democrat] Al Smith—because Smith was Catholic—when he ran for president in 1928, that he used to say, "Politics is dirty business, you ought to stay out of it." So he didn't encourage me to get involved in politics—just the opposite.

But I did get involved, almost the moment I stepped on campus at the University of Wisconsin. Of course, for a kid from Burlington, a small agricultural town—I think there were fifty-seven kids in my high school graduation class and only three or four of us went on to college—all boys. Girls from Burlington simply didn't go to college for the most part at that time.

I was thrilled, of course, to come to Madison and see this great big university. And I remember the president of the student body spoke at the old Stock Pavilion shortly after I got there, and I thought, Man, that's what I want to do—get involved in student politics and see what we could accomplish.

ZALESKI: That was the spark?

GARVEY: It was. I started getting involved in elections at the student senate level, that sort of thing. But I also had a great deal of interest in what was happening at the national level.

A Wisconsin Congressman, Henry Reuss, had started a program similar to the Peace Corps that was called the Point Four Youth Corps. There was a great deal of excitement among students that you could join the corps some day and do some good in the world.

And we met Hubert Humphrey and Eleanor Roosevelt and Ralph Bunche [the first person of color to win the Nobel Peace Prize], mainly through the National Student Association [NSA]. For example, I went to Hyde Park in New York with a group of students from around the country for an NSA Congress. And while we were there, suddenly this voice says, "Well, hello young men!" And I turned and it was Eleanor Roosevelt. And I remember going, "Whoa! Get serious here, folks." She took us on a tour and then gave us a lecture. She emphasized that we weren't in college to have a good time, that we needed to do something worthwhile. It was quite impressive.

So when you ask about liberal heroes, Eleanor certainly would be on that list. Later on, of course, I admired John and Bobby Kennedy, Martin Luther King, Gene McCarthy, Hubert Humphrey. And more recently, the late Senator Paul Wellstone of Minnesota and Senator Bernie Sanders of Vermont.

ZALESKI: Who inspired you the most?

GARVEY: Well, in my world nobody can top [former Wisconsin governor and senator] Gaylord Nelson. He was my mentor. I loved that guy. I met him while serving in student government when he was governor of Wisconsin. And then when I ran for the U.S. Senate against [Bob] Kasten in 1986, I sought Gaylord's advice and he was quite helpful. He'd lost his Senate seat to Kasten in 1980—what a tragedy that was—and wanted to see Kasten defeated in the worst way.

ZALESKI: What was it about Nelson that impressed you—his style, his beliefs, his environmental credentials?

GARVEY: Well, he was extremely bright and one of the best public speakers I've ever heard. He was also one of the funniest people I've ever met and just a terrific human being.

ZALESKI: Why, in your opinion, was he so widely admired and able to serve as long as he did?

GARVEY: Well, to some extent, everything is timing, right? I mean, Gaylord Nelson and Judge James Doyle [father of recent Wisconsin governor Jim Doyle Jr.] and Patrick Lucey and a few others started the new Wisconsin Democratic Party, really. They took over the party in 1948, and Gaylord won a seat in the state senate. And two years after that, he ran for the U.S. Senate and won that, too.

And once there he became a great progressive leader, one of the most effective senators in our country's history. And it wasn't just that he was the father of Earth Day that made him stand out—his list of accomplishments goes on and on. And other members of the Senate loved Gaylord even if they disagreed with his politics.

ZALESKI: You've mentioned how close the two of you were. Any stories come to mind—humorous or otherwise?

GARVEY: Most of them were situational, just things that would come up. But here's one: when Gaylord was running for reelection to the U.S. Senate in 1980, he decided to take a train from Kenosha to northern Wisconsin. Bronson La Follette was running for governor at the time, and I was working for Bronson's campaign.

So Bronson told me, "Ed, your task is to make sure there are some La Follette signs on that train so that when it goes through the state, people will be reminded that La Follette is running as well." So I got a bunch of volunteers, and at about 3 a.m. we went down to the train station and put La Follette posters all over the train. When Gaylord and his staff got to the train that morning, it looked like the La Follette train—oh, and by the way, we're going to let Gaylord get on, too. [Laughs.] Gaylord's staff was furious, but Gaylord thought it was a riot— just very funny. And he came over to me and said, "Ed, you don't mind if I put up just one sign, do you?"

History will remember him well—Earth Day, his progressive politics, his sense of humor.

6

Civil Rights

While he took enormous pride in his myriad accomplishments, Garvey saw himself first and foremost as a champion of civil rights. It was, he emphasized near the end of our previous session, how he wanted to be remembered: as someone who spent his entire adult life fighting racial injustice. He was incredulous that—a century and a half after the Civil War ended—many white Americans still harbored intense hatred toward African Americans. And, in some cases, refused to accept that slavery represented an abhorrent chapter in our nation's history.

So of all our sessions, none was greeted more enthusiastically by Garvey than the one that delved into his civil rights activism—which, he was quick to note, preceded some of the most horrific racial violence in U.S. history: notably, the 1963 bombing of the 16th Street Baptist Church in Birmingham, Alabama, that killed four young black girls and the grisly murders of three young white civil rights workers near Philadelphia, Mississippi, in June 1964—one of whom, Andrew Goodman, had attended the University of Wisconsin. We talked for a little more than an hour, and I never again saw him as emotionally charged and animated as he was that morning.

●

ZALESKI: We've talked about how you first began dabbling in politics while in college. That's also the first time you had a conversation with a black person, correct?

GARVEY: Yeah, at the National Student Association Congress in Champagne-Urbana, Illinois. I was standing in line in the cafeteria and there was this black fellow behind me, and I said, "Do you mind if I have lunch with you?" He said "No, I don't mind." And I told him, "I've never talked to a Negro before, and I'd like to do that." And he said, "Well, I'm your man."

So we sat down and started talking and developed a nice relationship. I guess what I got out of it was how important it is to communicate and be given a different perspective. For example, at that time Americans were still pretty proud of the Supreme Court's *Brown vs. Board of Education* in 1954 that banned segregated schools. But as this fellow pointed out, his kids would probably be out of grade school before it was fully implemented because of the wording of the decision—"with all deliberate speed."

So it gave me a different perspective on how you look at issues like school integration, whether you're black or whether you're white. I also remember a speech that was given at that congress, the title of which was "How an Atheist Will Face God." It raised the question, "If a Southern white goes to heaven and there's a God, but God is a black man or a black woman, what are they going to do?" So it was sort of a jarring experience for me at that time. But it was clear by the time I left that congress that civil rights was going to be an important part of my life. I just felt it.

ZALESKI: When did you start leaning left politically?

GARVEY: When I joined student government at the University of Wisconsin, really, and the NSA, primarily. Everybody who was involved with the NSA was liberal—well, not everybody, but almost everybody. And it was right around that time that William F. Buckley started the conservative Young Americans for Freedom, which would attack us as communists and so forth.

I remember we had the NSA Congress in Madison in 1961, and Buckley came here to urge students to withdraw from the NSA because he said we were so far to the left we were essentially pinkos. It was also the period in history when the sit-ins were beginning in the South and you had the Freedom Ride, and there was this ferment on the campuses that civil rights was moving to the front of all other issues.

So here was William Buckley telling students to get away from the NSA because we were too far to the left, and so forth—caring not one whit about what was going on with black students either in the North or the South.

In my junior year I was elected student body president, and the sit-ins had just begun in Greensboro, North Carolina. So the student senate at the UW invited students from Fisk University, a black college in Tennessee, to take buses that we chartered to Madison to speak to our student senate about what was going on down there.

So they came here and we all sang "We Shall Overcome," and then we all marched to the Capitol and picketed Woolworth's, which was across the street on the Capitol Square, because the Woolworth's down South all had segregated lunch counters.

ZALESKI: Your first taste of real activism?

GARVEY: Right. And when we got to the store, the people there were saying, "Why are you picketing here—why don't you go down South and picket?" And we said, "Well, because you're all part of the same chain and your company ought to stop discriminating."

And just doing that and talking to these kids my age, who were participating in nonviolent protests, sitting in and being beaten up, thrown in jail, having cigarettes snuffed out on their backs, whatever, it was a life-changing event for me. Because I saw that this took enormous courage on the part of these young people who were risking their lives, really, for the right to do things that white people could do automatically.

ZALESKI: Another life-changing event was going to Jackson, Mississippi, just as the civil rights movement was heating up in 1961. How did that come about?

GARVEY: When I ran for president at that NSA Congress right after we graduated, civil rights was a major focus. I was elected SNC [Student Nonviolent Committee] president in August 1961, and the first SNC event I ever attended was in Jackson, Mississippi, in September 1961.

I got on the plane—alone—and flew to Jackson. And I remember the cab driver saying, "Where to?" and I gave him the address and he said, "You mean you want to go down there with those niggers?" And I said, "No, I want to go down there and meet with the Student Nonviolent Coordinating Committee." And he said, "Yeah, the niggers." And I thought, what do you do at this point? So I said, "Just take me." So he drove me there, and I gave him a nickel for a tip.

ZALESKI: A precursor of sorts?

GARVEY: Yeah. And it was interesting because we all stayed with black families. It was just a totally different experience for me as a young twenty-one-year-old white kid going to Jackson, Mississippi. And on the second day of the SNC meetings, the police came to the door and told us that the restaurant across the street—which was owned by blacks—was no longer integrated, and that any whites who went there would be arrested.

So we discussed what we should do and again sang "We Shall Overcome," and decided that we should go across the street, past the police dogs, and into the restaurant. I can't remember exactly, but there must have been fifteen or twenty of us.

ZALESKI: Police dogs—meaning German shepherds. Obviously a terrifying moment.

GARVEY: Whoa! I've never been so scared in my life! I mean, we're walking out singing, "We are not afraid," and here are these German shepherds, teeth bared, and all these cops in riot gear, and I thought, oh my God, this is not going to be a good time. I mean, I was sure I was going to end up in jail, and I was just hoping they weren't going to release the dogs. [Smiles.]

I've never liked German shepherds since—Oh Jesus, no thanks. But they didn't release the dogs, and they didn't arrest us. And as we sat around and talked about it later, we decided the reason was that the cops were confused and couldn't comprehend why a white person would want to eat in a black restaurant. Because the whole point of segregation was to keep the blacks out of the white restaurants.

So we decided it was either too embarrassing for them or they weren't organized and weren't prepared for that. But keep in mind this was 1961—so it was still quite a long time before the stuff you saw in *Mississippi Burning*.

But it was a tough time, and people in the restaurant— middle-aged blacks in particular—said to us, "You know, you really shouldn't be down here stirring things up, because we haven't had a lynching in several months." So their attitude was, are you sure you want to be down here? Because the white people down here are going to get pretty ticked off if you hassle them. And you had to sort of ask yourself, were we doing good or bad by being there? What was the deal?

And right after that I went to Baton Rouge, Louisiana, which had been shut down because of civil rights activity, and the white leaders in the community said nobody should be allowed on the Louisiana State campus. Looking back now, I was just incredibly lucky. But those kinds of experience shape your life.

ZALESKI: And it was during this period that you met the Reverend Martin Luther King?

GARVEY: That's right. He met us for lunch at the YWCA in Atlanta that same year—1961. And we thought he was a very conservative minister who was standing in the way. We thought he was a problem, because we felt that with the sit-ins and wait-ins and all this other stuff we would change the South immediately. And King, of course, knew that this was going to be a long struggle and that you had to get the black middle-class and the black churches involved in the movement. But we thought King was way too conservative.

ZALESKI: So you had no inkling that this man was about to become the most celebrated and revered civil rights figure of our time?

GARVEY: No. He was just another minister. We knew his reputation was growing, but no, I wasn't impressed. In retrospect, I wish I'd had the foresight to really think about it so that I could have asked him a lot of questions. But now, looking back, I'm just happy to have met him.

7

MAYHEM IN CHICAGO

If there was one event in the sixties that opened Garvey's eyes—and nearly his skull—about how divided the country had become and that it was careening out of control, it was the chaotic Democratic National Convention in Chicago in August 1968. Forty years later, the memories of the beatings that an enraged force of twenty-three thousand police and National Guardsmen—egged on by Chicago Mayor Richard Daley—administered to a crowd of ten thousand Vietnam War protestors and assorted media representatives were still seared in his psyche.

It was his first awareness, he said, of the lengths to which some politicians will go in order to maintain power—even if, as in this case, the bloody spectacle was being beamed into living rooms across the nation.

The confrontation, in the late afternoon of August 28, occurred just months after the assassinations of Martin Luther King Jr. (in April) and Bobby Kennedy (in Los Angeles), both of which had ignited riots and civil unrest in dozens of American cities. And it cast an ugly shadow over the convention itself, during which Democrats—seemingly unmoved by the mayhem that was occurring just miles away—nominated as their presidential candidate Lyndon Johnson's vice president, Hubert Humphrey, whose stance on the war seemed to shift daily.

The carnage he witnessed that day, Garvey said, was the stuff of brutal dictatorships determined to silence their opponents—certainly not something you'd expect in the United States of America. It was an emotionally numbing experience that not only shook him to the core but helped prepare him psychologically for the many rough-and-tumble battles that lay just ahead in his career.

●

ZALESKI: While attending the UW Law School, you spent the tumultuous summer of 1968 working in the Chicago police department's civil rights division during the infamous Democratic National Convention there. So you witnessed the protests and the so-called police riot up close. How did that come about?

GARVEY: Well, Herman Goldstein and Frank Remington, both law school professors, had this program with the Ford Foundation in which law students would go to a major city and ride along with the police so they could get a better idea of what life was like in the streets. And yes, as it happened, I was assigned to the civil rights desk of the Chicago police department during the '68 convention.

Its role was to avoid confrontation with the hippies and so forth. So we'd go out with the police and have conversations with the Vietnam War protestors to make sure the lines of communication were open so the city could avoid any needless violence.

Then all of a sudden, in the middle of the convention, the word came down from Mayor Daley's office that there'd be no more discussions, that this was going to be a military response [to the protests] and not a typical discussion.

ZALESKI: What initiated it?

GARVEY: Daley was angry about the way the media was covering the convention and his role in the whole thing—and he decided it was payback time. So our people—those working on the civil rights desk—were assigned to twelve-hour shifts with everybody else. We drove around on reserve police buses and stuff like that. And one night the cop I was with drove to Grant Park and Lincoln Park and then out to the International Amphitheatre, where the convention was being held, in an unmarked car to see what was going on.

We kept hearing that the cops had been told to beat up the TV reporters and smash their cameras, so we went around warning the TV people that they should have some extra security. But they didn't believe it. And shortly after, of course, the police busted up their cameras and roughed up some people.

ZALESKI: Did you actually witness reporters getting pummeled?

GARVEY: Yeah, in Grant Park. In fact, I was taking pictures of one of the cops hammering a guy with a night stick and a cop came roaring up on a three-wheeler and practically ran me over. The cop I was with grabbed me by the back of my shirt and my belt and just yanked me back. It was a close call. And then we took off running across Michigan Avenue and got back into his car.

But yeah, we saw the stuff that was going on. And when the media called it a police riot, well, that's what it was. When I finally returned to Madison, I stopped in Burlington on the way home to see my parents. And I told them I thought it was the end of democracy, because what had happened clearly was not an exercise in democracy. It was a way for the Chicago police to suppress people, and I'll tell you, it was pretty frightening stuff.

So when the Walker Commission [an investigation led by Daniel Walker, head of the Chicago Crime Commission] later came out with its report and agreed that it had been a police riot, I can tell you it was absolutely true. Except that the word riot suggests mayhem. This was much more programmed than that—although it was clearly an effort to suppress the free speech rights of people who were protesting.

ZALESKI: It was downright shocking for those of us who watched it on TV.

GARVEY: Right. And before the convention that summer our job was to go into all white sections of Chicago where black families were moving in to try to reduce the tension between blacks and whites. And it was a real eye-opener, because as bad as things had been in the South—in Jackson, Mississippi, for example—the hatred expressed in these neighborhoods was staggering.

You'd be talking to people, and I remember this one white woman, who had a job as a pet groomer, said, "You've got to come with me because the bus is arriving over at the school." The city was bussing in black kids, probably four or five years old, for summer programs, and these people were out there standing and shouting at these little kids as they got off the bus, "Nigger! Nigger! Nigger!" And I'm screaming, "Stop it! What the hell's wrong with you?" And they'd just continue, "Nigger! Nigger! Nigger!" The cops told me later that when Martin Luther King had come through these neighborhoods, he and his people were scared out of their wits because they thought they were going to be attacked by these crowds. So, yeah, those were tough times.

The cops said some people on the north side of Chicago had put up pictures of King, only they called him Martin Lucifer

King. And the pictures had horns coming out and a tail and the whole thing—the hatred was just phenomenal. I'd never heard people yelling racist stuff at little kids. It was like, "C'mon, what the hell's going on here?"

I mean, you wanted to say, "Look, there are some rules we've got to follow here, folks, and one of them is we're not going to poison the minds of little kids." So I think the [1961] Sidney Poitier movie, *Raisin in the Sun*, was a good primer for what was going on there.

Chicago was a great experience for a number of reasons, one being that we saw what police will do when the civil authorities decide they're going to clamp down—if they can get away with it. And to see the outward racism and the willingness to express it by people who don't care what anyone else thinks . . . it was quite an experience.

ZALESKI: So this was another transformative moment for you?

GARVEY: Exactly. A moment where you have to sort of say, "Ok, so what the hell's the lesson here?" And I took the lesson to be that you have to elect people to public office who really believe in civil rights and are willing to take some risks for civil rights and call people out on it. So I thought the Walker Commission was terrific because it did take on the power structure and say, this crap cannot be tolerated.

8

THE TUMULTUOUS SIXTIES

Like most Americans who grew up in the sixties—whether in isolated, rural white towns or in teeming, diverse big cities—Garvey was jolted by the seemingly endless stream of harrowing events that came to symbolize that decade. One didn't experience the sixties, one survived them, he recalled with a shudder. And he agreed that many young people today don't seem to grasp just how unsettling that decade was.

Indeed, anyone who came of age during that era can recall not only where they were during the 1962 Cuban Missile Crisis—in many instances, hiding under the covers, pondering what it would be like to be incinerated in a nuclear holocaust—but also their reactions to the assassinations of first John Kennedy, then Martin Luther King, and finally John's brother Bobby—all within the span of five years.

I still vividly remember wandering half-asleep into our living room the morning of June 6, 1968, and seeing my family solemnly huddled around the TV. I was a twenty-year-old sophomore at UW–Milwaukee and about to begin a summer job helping repair softball fields in the inner-city—and I re-member bracing for more horrible news.

After a few moments of uneasy silence, I sputtered, "Now what?!!" My sister LeeAnne turned to me teary-eyed and re-plied, "Bobby Kennedy was assassinated last night in Los Angeles." With that, I left the room, grabbed my basketball, bolted for the back door and jogged trance-like to Fernwood Elementary School. I spent the next hour there shooting bas-kets, alone, wondering how many more tragedies our country could possibly endure.

And, as Garvey pointed out, the Martin Luther King and Bobby Kennedy murders occurred at a time when families in cities large and small were being torn apart by the escalation of the Vietnam War.

But as agonizing as that decade was, Garvey felt com-pelled to talk about it, largely because the events of that period had steered the country in a sharply different direc-tion. They also, he made clear, left an indelible mark on Ed Garvey the emerging progressive activist.

●

ZALESKI: You've mentioned being an MP [military police] in the army at Fort Gordon, Georgia, when JFK was assassi-nated in 1963. How did you view him at the time?

GARVEY: Well, I thought Kennedy—like Martin Luther King—was a little too conservative during that period. I thought he should be supporting national health care and not just Medicare and Medicaid.

I had gone through the ROTC [Reserve Officer Training Corps] at the UW—it was mandatory for young men coming to the university to take two years of ROTC training back then. Then there was an advanced ROTC program in your junior and senior year where you could then graduate as a second lieutenant. You also got paid about $30 a month, so I was de-lighted to join the advanced program to get that extra $30 a month so I could take Betty to lunch or whatever.

So I entered the army as a second lieutenant at Fort Gordon when Kennedy was shot, and I remember the local TV stations down there had "Man on the Street" interviews in the city. And I'd say that five out of six of those interviewed said they were happy that Kennedy had been killed.

Of course, the next night the TV station interviewed a rabbi and a minister and a priest, all saying the people quoted the day before didn't represent the good people of Augusta, Geor-gia. The hell they didn't! They said exactly what they thought! Remember, this was the South, 1963.

ZALESKI: How did the assassination affect you?

GARVEY: Pretty dramatically. You just couldn't believe it happened. Everything sort of stopped.

We were at this army base and we'd spend our time watch-ing TV newscasts of the whole thing. We were watching when [Lee Harvey] Oswald was shot and killed by Jack Ruby. And we were thinking, Jesus, what's going on here? You really started to question who's in charge of the government and what was happening—was it a lone assassin or was it more than that? And who was this Jack Ruby? I mean, for heaven's sakes, how does this guy get into the Dallas police station to shoot Oswald? None of it made any sense.

ZALESKI: A half-century later, do you think Oswald acted alone?

GARVEY: I find it hard to believe. There's no question he was involved, but it just doesn't add up. The pristine bullet they found on Kennedy's stretcher at the hospital, the whole thing.

I don't sit around and think about it that much but it's also hard for me to believe that a single assassin was responsible for Bobby Kennedy's death. He was supposed to go out the front of the Ambassador Hotel, after the election victory in the California primary, and at the last minute an FBI agent tells him you're going to go through the kitchen instead? And Sirhan Sirhan is waiting there with a gun? I mean, how lucky can you be, Sirhan?

And King the same thing. It just seems hard to believe that these were all cases of lone assassins. It's possible, but I find it difficult to accept.

ZALESKI: You mentioned that you revered Bobby Kennedy. Why is that?

GARVEY: Well, I met both Bobby and JFK when John was running for president in 1960. They came to the UW campus, and in those days we had mock political conventions, and I was the head of that. And we had a rule that the candidates themselves couldn't appear, that the students had to do the work.

But Bobby Kennedy came to the campus and I met him and told him what the rules were, and he said, "Well, I'd really like to have a chance to speak. And I won't mention the campaign." When I mentioned it to our faculty adviser, he said, "Ed, that's not allowed—you can't let him speak." And I said, "Oh, c'mon, everybody wants to hear Bobby Kennedy speak. Besides, he's not going to talk about the campaign."

So we introduced Bobby at Tripp Commons at the UW Memorial Union. And he told the crowd, "I know what your rules are. I can't talk about candidates, and I can't talk about the election. I just want to tell you about the author of a book called *Profiles in Courage*"—which, of course, was John. And as he proceeded to talk about John's background, the faculty adviser went nuts.

ZALESKI: Much to your delight, I presume?

GARVEY: Oh, of course. And when it was over, I stood with Bobby at the top of the steps at the student union, and he asked me if I'd drop out of school and work for the campaign. And I said, no, because my parents would have gone into cardiac arrest if I dropped out of school and got involved in politics.

So I remember watching Bobby skip down the steps of the Memorial Union and thinking, I'm not sure that was the right answer. Maybe I should quit school and join the campaign. But Bobby became sort of a hero of mine for a number of different reasons.

ZALESKI: What about John Kennedy?

GARVEY: JFK was exciting, dynamic, alive. He changed politics, changed the whole attitude of the country with his great inaugural address. I was lucky to meet both of them.

ZALESKI: But you found Bobby more inspiring?

GARVEY: I did, and probably because of the circumstances. Understand, I was still evolving at that point—and to some extent I think the Kennedys were too, because John Kennedy wasn't exactly at the forefront of the civil rights movement in 1960. And Bobby was coming along behind him and was much more involved. And I found Bobby to be one of the more interesting people I've ever come across.

ZALESKI: Where were you when Bobby was shot?

GARVEY: In law school here at the UW. I'd been asked to start opening some offices in Wisconsin for Bobby's presidential campaign and was just about to do that.

I remember the night he was assassinated, Betty had gone to bed—we were living in student housing at Eagle Heights at the time. She was pregnant with Kathleen, our second child, and I'd stayed up to watch the election returns from the Democratic primary in California, which Bobby won.

I was so thrilled with Bobby's speech after the victory, and I couldn't wait for Betty to wake up the next morning to tell her. So I went to bed, and then the phone rang at around 6 a.m. It was a friend, and he said, "Did you hear the news? Bobby's been shot." And I thought, oh Christ!

I was just devastated—Betty and I both were. Because we had opted for Bobby over Gene McCarthy, who was also running for the Democratic nomination.

We felt Bobby was the only one who could get us out of the Vietnam War. I mean, we supported Bobby for a whole variety of things—from civil rights to the war. We felt his campaign was what this country was all about.

ZALESKI: Just two months prior to that, Martin Luther King was assassinated in Memphis. I presume your opinion of him had changed by then?

GARVEY: Oh God, yes! I mean, he was one of the major figures of our time. And smartass me, to think that back in '61 I thought he was just a conservative minister.

ZALESKI: Reflecting on it now, do you think the upheaval of the sixties influenced the path you took with your life?

GARVEY: Oh, without question. But, you know, I took my grandson to the Super Bowl in Dallas earlier this year, and while we were there we visited the Sixth Floor Museum in Dealey Plaza, where John's assassination took place. And I couldn't finish the tour—I just couldn't take it. It affected me so much I had to leave the building. I just found it so disturbing to dredge up all those bad memories. It brought back everything—not just John Kennedy's assassination but Bobby Kennedy's and Martin Luther King's and Malcolm X's. You forget sometimes what a horrific few years those were.

9

THE CIA SURPRISE

After we had completed our interview on the lasting impact of the sixties, I suddenly remembered Ed mentioning in our very first interview that he couldn't wait to tell me about his involvement with the CIA. He said it with a cackle, so I wasn't sure what to make of it.

But as I turned off my recorder and got up to leave, I reminded him of his earlier comment and he started chuckling. Then he asked that I sit back down for a few more minutes so he could regale me about one of the most bizarre episodes of his life.

●

ZALESKI: You mentioned earlier that at some point we should probably talk about your links to the CIA. At first I thought you were you joking—but this actually happened?

GARVEY: Oh yeah. But it's pretty crazy. While I was attending the UW, I was elected president of the National Student Association [NSA, in 1963]. And one day I got a phone call from a former NSA officer who asked if I'd like to go to the White

House and meet Ralph Dungan, a special assistant for President Kennedy. I said, "Hey, I'm from Burlington, Wisconsin—would I like to go to the White House?"

So I got on the train at the 30th Street Station in Philadelphia and went to Washington. Then I got in a cab and, for the first and last time of my life, I said, "Take me to the White House." So I get to the White House and meet with Dungan, and he tells me how much President Kennedy thinks of the NSA and that they were supporting our efforts against William Buckley and Fulton Lewis III [national field director for a conservative youth group], who were trying to get schools to disaffiliate with our association.

Dungan said if I needed a photo of the president or Bobby Kennedy or Arthur Goldberg to help convince students they should be part of NSA, he'd be happy to arrange it. Then he gave me a tour of the oval office and all that stuff.

I even saw the cleat marks from the president's desk to the putting green outside. Dungan said that when Ike was president, he'd put on his golf shoes at the desk and then walk outside to practice his putting stroke.

Anyway, Dungan arranged for a car to pick me up, and I just remember being so excited even though I had no idea what he had planned for me next. So I asked him, "Where am I going?" And he said, "Well, I met somebody who wants to give some money to the NSA's international program."

So I'm thinking, Wow, what a day! First the White House, then I have my picture taken with Bobby and the president and Arthur Goldberg, and I find out the president really cares about the NSA and thinks it's an important institution. And now I'm going to meet somebody who wants to give us money for our international program?

So we drive to this apartment building and go up to whatever floor it was and Dungan introduces me to a Mr. Green, who invites me in. And Dungan says, "I have an errand to run, I'll be back in about half an hour."

So I sit down and this Mr. Green says, "Do you have any problem talking to someone from the federal government?" I said, "Uh, I've just been to the White House. I mean, excuse me, do you know who I am?"

So he smiles back and says, "Where does the NSA get its money?" And I said, "Well, there's the San Jacinto Fund in Texas, the Independence Foundation in Boston, and the Foundation for Youth and Student Affairs in New York."

He said, "Well, I have some information for you but you have to sign this secrecy agreement before I can tell you." He said it didn't obligate me to do anything except keep quiet about this conversation.

ZALESKI: And, naturally, you signed it.

GARVEY: Right. Then he tells me, "The money is actually coming from the Central Intelligence Agency, going through these foundations." You could have knocked me over with a feather.

I said, "Are you kidding?" He said, "No. During the Joe McCarthy period, the State Department could never send students abroad because McCarthy would say, 'They're communists, blah, blah, blah.'" So all the good guys left the State Department and joined the CIA. And they work with student leaders, labor leaders, and others to push democracy, particularly in the Third World. "And so," he said, "that money is coming from the CIA. But the CIA will not try to steer you in any direction."

ZALESKI: Who was this guy—and what was his title?

GARVEY: I didn't know who he was, except that he was an official of the U.S. government. So he says, "You should talk to some other past NSA officers so you can rest assured that we're not trying to manipulate you in any way. We're just providing the money so you can do things abroad because we think that the antidote to communism is free expression of ideas from people from the West, and we want to get students from Latin America and Asia and Africa to come to the United States and go through our programs and so on."

And since [the NSA] was fighting the Portuguese at the student level, working with the Angolan and Mozambiquen student leaders opposed to Portuguese rule, and working with South African students against the South African government, and so on . . . I mean, we were doing all the things that lefties dream to do. And this Mr. Green said, "That won't change. I mean, that's your policies. And, in fact, it's probably better because you're often times taking positions that are contrary to the best interests of the United States, because you'll be more effective in the Third World. So you can't tell anybody."

So I get in the cab and I go to the train station. I'm taking the train back to Philadelphia, where Betty is waiting for me at our apartment. And I'm not supposed to tell her? So, of course, the first thing I say as I walk into our apartment, "Betty, guess what? It's the CIA!" She goes, "What?!!?" "It's the CIA [that's funding the NSA]!"

One of the things that I was assured of that day was that Bobby Kennedy was in charge of the program—or he oversaw it. And so the coordination within the government itself was under Bobby's guidance.

ZALESKI: Bobby Kennedy essentially was running the NSA's international program with funding from the CIA?

GARVEY: Hell, yeah, that's what was going on. Listen, looking back now, I don't know. Was I doing the right thing, the wrong thing?

ZALESKI: In other words, this was the sort of shadowy stuff people hear about but have no idea if it's real or not.

GARVEY: Well, and you *don't* know. You're told the information doesn't go beyond the good guys. And because we
were doing things like helping the South Africans and the
Rhodesians and the Mozambiquens . . .

When [Algerian Premier] Ahmed Ben Bella came to the
United States [in 1962] to appear at the United Nations because
Algeria had become a free country, he asked to see two people:
the president and the international affairs vice president of
the NSA. So we go to New York to meet with Ben Bella and
Mohammad Khemisti, his former minister of foreign affairs, in
a hotel suite. And here I'm twenty-one, and Ben Bella is thank-
ing me because we've helped him by providing scholarships
for Algerian students so they could come back and be better
leaders. That's not heady stuff, is it? [Editor's note: Ben Bella
was overthrown in 1965.]

So I'm thinking, here's Fulton Lewis III and Bill Buckley
thinking we're communists—and we're actually working for a
program that's certainly suspect by everybody of my political
persuasion.

ZALESKI: Very bizarre, to say the least.

GARVEY: And the reason I can talk about it now is, it ultimately all came out in *Ramparts* magazine [in 1967]. One of the
guys who'd been a president of NSA talked to *Ramparts* and
blew the whistle on the CIA's involvement. And so then it became a cause célèbre, and it was just a question of when the
other shoe was going to fall.

We knew that Hughes Rudd was going to be the first one to
announce it on TV, on the *CBS Morning News,* a short time
later. And so Hughes Rudd reports that the CIA has been involved in supporting this "subversive NSA blah, blah, blah."
And, of course, all the government officials were like, "What?
We didn't know anything about it. This is an outrage!"

One guy stood up for the NSA—Bobby Kennedy. He went

on *Meet the Press* and said, "These young people risked their lives for this country and they thought they were doing the right thing."

Everybody else ran for cover. And I'm saying to myself, "Who needs this?" Because you can imagine all the conflicting things that are going on here. I mean, were we doing the right thing? The wrong thing? And so for Bobby to stand up for us was quite remarkable.

ZALESKI: Which explains why he's one of your heroes?

GARVEY: Oh yeah. And he was pretty high up there anyway. When I decided to run against Kasten [in 1986], the first thing I did was convene a meeting among all the lefties in my campaign over at [campaign manager Bill] Christofferson's house. And I brought along the *Ramparts* magazine article. And I said, "I want you all to know that I knew [about the CIA's involvement]." Because most people in that situation would say, "Well, you can just deny it. You didn't know." I said, "No, I knew." Because the presidents of NSA all agreed that we would take the hit. And that would stop the story there, and it would not go beyond other people who were involved.

So I said to this group of campaign workers, "If you think this disqualifies me to run, say so now." And this one guy says, "Well, in those days wasn't everybody involved with the CIA?" I said, "Not everybody—there were a few people who weren't." And everyone laughed. And that was end of it.

Shaking Up the NFL

Although his NFLPA days seemed like eons ago, there was little question during our interviews that the memories and accomplishments from that twelve-year period—especially in the beginning, when he unarguably was one of the most detested men in America, at least in the eyes of pro football fans—were still a vital part of his identity. I also got the sense that he felt his unyielding role in forcing NFL owners to eventually sit down and bargain with the union and share in their largesse is still underappreciated by the media and the sporting public in general.

While the NFLPA didn't fully achieve its goals under Garvey, its two strikes during that period—in 1974 and 1982—garnered national headlines. And the second one—which lasted fifty-seven days and forced the league to shorten the season from sixteen to nine games—led to an agreement in which the players received 55 percent of the league's gross revenues.

Perhaps even more significant, in 1976 the Supreme Court upheld a lawsuit the union filed against the owners (*Mackey vs. NFL)* that argued the league's so-called Rozelle Rule violated antitrust laws by limiting a player's ability to act as a free agent. (After Garvey's death, DeMaurice Smith, the NFLPA's current executive director, said in a video on the union's website that Garvey had successfully challenged the league's "right to own men.")

As he reflected on that period, Garvey was troubled and mystified that so many people still resented pro football players making millions of dollars for, in essence, playing a game. Why, he barked, should team owners be the only ones richly compensated, when it was the players who risked life and limb—and, we realize now, their brains—every time they stepped foot on a playing field? And why couldn't fans appreciate, he exclaimed, that it's the players who were chiefly responsible for pro football becoming the hottest and most lucrative sports enterprise in the country?

This session lasted more than ninety minutes, and he was firing on all cylinders the moment I walked through the door. The NFL, Ed asserted, wouldn't be where it is today if it weren't for the bold, brave individuals who created the players union in 1956 and then, beginning with his hiring as executive director in 1971, aggressively promoted the right to its existence. (The NFLPA and the old American Football League Players Association, established in 1964, joined forces after the leagues merged in 1970.) It's a big part of his legacy—and one that only in recent years has come into focus.

●

ZALESKI: After you got your law degree, you and Betty moved to Minneapolis so you could go to work for a prestigious, liberal law firm. But you were there only four months before you were assigned to counsel John Mackey, president of the National Football League Players Association. And just a year after that, 1971, you became the group's executive director—and almost overnight became one of the most reviled figures in America: a brazen, long-haired thirty-one-year-old lawyer from a small town in Wisconsin. People just couldn't accept the idea that pro athletes should be paid big money to play football—a kid's game, for cripes' sake. Why did you do it?

GARVEY: Actually, when I took the job, the average salary in the National Football League was about $24,000. So it was more than the average worker, but not exponentially more.

ZALESKI: I remember reading that when the Packers won their first Super Bowl in 1966, only one offensive lineman, apparently—Forrest Gregg—made over $20,000.

GARVEY: I'm not sure if that's true, but Packer fans all know the story of Jim Ringo, the all-pro center, who went to [Coach Vince] Lombardi and demanded a raise and was immediately traded to Philadelphia. [Former Packer center] Ken Bowman tells a similar story. He asked for a meeting with Lombardi, and Lombardi said, "What do you want?" Bowman said he'd like to negotiate his salary. Lombardi glared at him and said, "Son, you're lucky to be playing for the Green Bay Packers. What do you want?" Bowman said, "$24,000." Lombardi reached into his desk drawer and said, "Here's Forrest Gregg's contract. He's the best football player we've ever had. Take a look, he's only making $24,500. You have the nerve to come in here and tell me you're worth as much as Forrest Gregg? Son, you're lucky to be on this team. You'd better leave." And Bowman said, "Ah, yes sir."

But when I joined the players union, we thought that if we could just get lawyers to represent players in those negotiations maybe that would even the odds a bit. The system was screwing the players, not the individual situations. Players didn't have any rights at all.

What angered people like Dave Anderson [sports columnist for the *New York Times*] was the idea that the players *deserved* any rights. For some reason, the sports media seemed to like baseball and baseball players. But they didn't seem to like football and football players. Now part of it was a subtle racism—there were many more blacks in football than in baseball. And the writers, being all white, felt more comfortable with the old boys from the South in baseball than they did with black guys from the streets of Los Angeles.

ZALESKI: In the eleven years I covered the Packers, I'd see it all the time—white reporters congregating around white athletes because they felt more comfortable with them. I always contended that a black athlete had to practically be a superstar to get any publicity—at least back in the 1970s.

GARVEY: Right. I mean, the fact that the National Football League was lily white when it was formed in 1921 and remained that way even after Jackie Robinson broke the color barrier in baseball [in 1947]—and the fact that you couldn't get any blacks hired as coaches and that the writers remained silent about that was mind-boggling to most of the players.

ZALESKI: Your first year with the NFLPA, 1971, had to be overwhelming. You were constantly being vilified—by the owners, the media, and the fans. And yet, I must say, you seemed to relish the confrontations.

GARVEY: Well, I was just out of UW Law School and was working with Leonard Lindquist, who was a great labor lawyer, on the player negotiations at that time. Leonard wasn't there one day when Howard Cosell, the famous TV commentator, came in to talk to the player negotiators at the Summit Hotel in New York. And the first thing Cosell did was take a long look at me. Then he turned to [former Baltimore Colts star and NFLPA president] John Mackey and said, "Who in the hell is this?" Mackey said, "He's our new labor lawyer."

Ed with daughter Pam and wife Betty at a rally for Senator George McGovern, the Democratic Party's 1972 presidential nominee versus Richard Nixon. (Garvey family photo)

And Cosell groaned and said, "Jesus Christ, I know more about labor law than he'll ever know. You don't need to talk to him, you can talk to me." [Laughs.]

And Mackey said, "Thanks, Howard, but if you don't mind we're going to use Ed." So Cosell turned to me and said, "What the hell do you know about labor?" And I replied, "Well, not as much as you sir, but I'll do my best." That was my introduction to Howard Cosell.

ZALESKI: And how did you get along with him after that?

GARVEY: Great. He was one of the few in the TV industry who really wanted to know what was going on. He actually came to Madison a few times and spoke on my behalf after I left the players' union.

ZALESKI: Cosell was even more controversial than you—people either loved or hated him. How would you describe him?

GARVEY: He was contentious, arrogant, bright. Great sense of humor. First time he came here, I met him at the Sheraton [Hotel], and we went up to his room. And the moment we get in the room, he calls his wife and tells her, "You're not going to believe this, but Ed Garvey is outside the hotel with a picket sign that says, 'No Jews—keep the Jews in New York.'" And I just looked at him and said, "Howard, what the hell's the matter with you?"

ZALESKI: You had a brutal first couple years—the owners did everything they could to try to discredit you. What was that like?

GARVEY: Well, the owners were just angry that there was a union, and [NFL commissioner] Pete Rozelle was ticked off because he saw life as a teeter-totter. So if the players were up, the owners were down—that's how he tended to see things. Then here I come to represent the players, and he was denigrating me at every opportunity. And at the beginning, the owners wouldn't even allow me in the rooms where they held the negotiations. I had to sit out in the hall. So the players would take a break and they'd say to me, "Here's what's happening, what do you think?" Then they'd go back in and make their presentation.

It took a couple years before [New York Giants co-owner] Wellington Mara would sit in the same room with me. When we had federal mediation, I'd ask a question and [Dallas president and general manager] Tex Schramm would look at John Mackey and say, "Well, John, in answer to your question . . ." And Mackey would say, "Tex, I didn't ask you any question." And Schramm would say, "Well, John, in answer to your question . . ."

And Mackey would say, "No, Tex. Ed Garvey asked the question. Please answer Ed." "Well, John, I prefer talking to you." And John would say, "Well, I don't prefer talking to you. So I'm not going to answer anything until you talk to our lawyer." And Schramm would say, "Well, John, we're just not going to go down that path. You've got lawyers, they've got egos, and big egos cause big problems. Who needs it?" So yeah, those were interesting times.

ZALESKI: Did you ever feel intimidated?

GARVEY: No, never did. Ted Kheel was the league's labor counsel, and he was famous for negotiating contracts through the newspapers. But he was generally regarded as an outstanding arbitrator. So the first time I met with Kheel was in New York, and he said to me, "You know, Mr. Garvey, *New York* magazine just listed me as one of the ten most powerful men in New York." I said, "Really?" He said, "That's right." And I said, "Well, if one of the ten most powerful men in New York and one of the best-known communists from Burlington, Wisconsin, can't solve this problem, who can?" He laughed and said, "You're crazy." And I said, "Yeah, I probably am."

ZALESKI: What was the biggest firestorm you encountered?

GARVEY: The rockiest period was probably 1975, after we'd lost three strikes in a row. And then we were resting all our eggs in one basket—namely the Mackey case against the NFL. If we'd lost that case at the district court level, then the union would have disappeared. So there was two years when the union didn't have automatic dues checkoff with the players' salaries—1972–73 and 1974–75. Which meant I had to go collect the union dues from individual players—just like Scott Walker has done with the teachers in Wisconsin.

At that point, we didn't know if we were going to survive or not. If we'd lost the Mackey case, the NFL would have moved in and squashed us. But we won, and the owners didn't

Ed and NFL Hall of Famer John Mackey, a former NFLPA president (*center*, with esteemed labor lawyer Leonard Lindquist), remained close friends until Mackey's death in 2011. Ed suspected that the head blows Mackey suffered in his football days were a major factor in his decline. (Garvey family photo)

know how to deal with it. So they appealed it to the U.S. Court of Appeals, and we won there, too. And when we won that, all of a sudden the owners said, "Well, maybe we should sit down and talk." But there were these moments when it could have been all over.

ZALESKI: Were there any owners you respected during that period?

GARVEY: Oh yeah—the Steelers' Dan Rooney. Every agreement that we reached, I reached it preliminarily with Rooney.

He was one of the old family owners. His father, Art, was also a good guy. I remember when I ran for the U.S. Senate in 1986, Art Rooney sent me $500. He said, "I don't agree with you on anything, but you're an honest man and you'll do a good job." I thought, wow, that's impressive.

ZALESKI: How were the owners of the Packers to deal with?

GARVEY: Terrible. We always thought the Packers would be better to deal with than the profit-oriented teams, but they never were. That said, not many people are aware that Bart Starr helped save us at one point.

ZALESKI: Bart Starr—conservative Republican Bart Starr?

GARVEY: Conservative Republican from Alabama. Yeah, that Bart Starr. It was 1970, and we were in the middle of negotiations with the owners, and Vince Lombardi—who'd just become coach of the Washington Redskins—had cancer. And apparently the doctors had operated and decided to close him back up—there was nothing they could do.

Rozelle met with [Pat] Richter and Mackey and Kermit Alexander [all NFLPA reps] and told them, "If Coach Lombardi dies and you're on strike, the owners will cancel the whole season. So I recommend that you have a meeting in Chicago. We'll pay for this, but each team will send four of their superstars to the meeting and you can decide what you want to do."

So John called me and asked, "What do you think?" I said, "I think it's pretty risky, because the owners will be picking the players." John said, "Well, we ought to be able to carry that day." So I said ok. John was supremely confident and one of the great leaders I've ever dealt with.

So we got to the Marriott Hotel in Chicago, and we sat down, and John outlined the situation and said he wanted to go around the room and get the players' input. And Johnny Unitas, the great Colts' quarterback, says, "Well, John Mackey, you're my leader but it's time to go to work. The pension's not that important, so I say, don't strike." Daryle Lamonica, quarterback of the Oakland Raiders, says, "I agree with Johnny. It's time to get back to work. We don't need this. It's not that important." Len Dawson of Kansas City, same thing. It gets to Bart Starr. He says, "Coach Lombardi hates unions, particularly this one. But he told me that if he were the quarterback of the Green Bay Packers, he would be a leader of the union."

Then Starr said, "I want you to know something. I make a lot more money because Ken Bowman is blocking for me. In fact, I make more than I should because of Ken. He's a player rep. I will not go to work until Ken Bowman tells me to go to work." And Unitas says, "Well, that's what I meant." And then the other players said, "We agree with Bart. Let's all vote together." And so we carried the day—thanks to Bart Starr.

I haven't told that story too often, but it was an amazing moment—almost unbelievable. And then the owners finally got serious about bargaining. Shortly after, we flew into New York and sat down and negotiated all night and came up with a collective bargaining agreement that year. But if Bart had jumped up and said he agreed with Unitas, Lamonica, and the others, we would have been toast. So I've always had great respect for Bart because he was willing to do that.

ZALESKI: That's a helluva story—one that I'm sure will shock many fans. Speaking of fans, how would you compare the public's perception of the NFLPA today versus forty years ago?

GARVEY: The biggest change is that when we first started the union in 1970, I think people felt we'd disappear. They didn't think we could survive against the all-powerful National Football League. Cosell used to say to me, "Their tentacles reach everywhere—they'll do everything they can to undermine

you. And you won't even know what happened." Today, I
don't think there's anybody who thinks that's the case.

ZALESKI: How bad did the animosity towards you get?
Were you ever threatened, punched? I know you experienced
considerable verbal abuse.

GARVEY: Oh yeah. When [Gene] Upshaw and I would be
walking up the street in New York, guys would be yelling out
their cars, all sorts of obscenities. And it was mostly directed
at me, of course, because Gene was a great athlete and fans, as
you know, tend to idolize the athletes no matter what. The guy
who's representing them, however, he's the guy you need to
be angry at.

Carroll Rosenbloom [former owner of the Los Angeles
Rams] once said to me during a phone conversation that for
$100 he could have me in the trunk of his car. And I said,
"Carroll, when I got out, I would blast you for fare-thee-well
to every newspaper in the country." He said, "I don't think
you know what I mean." And I said, "I don't think you know
how angry I would be." He said, "You're too stupid to talk to"
and hung up. So you had these moments. Mackey and some of
the other black players tended to think the owners were fully
capable of some violence.

ZALESKI: Any worrisome threats from fans?

GARVEY: Not really. There was the occasional nasty letter
sort of thing, saying, "Ed Garvey's a son of a bitch" or whatever. But no—not any actual threats.

The worst criticism probably came from the owners. After
Tex Schramm met me the first time, during a meeting in New
York with Rozelle, he went to back to Texas and called a meeting of team captains—all of whom were white, naturally, appointed by [Coach] Tom Landry. And Schramm told them that
he'd finally met their union head, Ed Garvey. And he said he

felt compelled to tell them that Garvey was a racist. And John Niland said, "Tex, c'mon, for God's sake, Mackey's one of Ed's best friends, so are [black players] Kermit Alexander and Alan Page. What are you talking about?" And Tex said, "That's my point. He hates white people!" And Niland said the captains threw things up in the air and said, "This meeting's over."

11

POLITICAL DEFEATS

Content that he'd laid the groundwork for the NFLPA to become even stronger, Garvey resigned as executive director and returned to Madison in 1983 to become assistant attorney general under Democrat Bronson La Follette. But he soon became antsy. He was dismayed not only by the direction the country was headed under President Ronald Reagan but by the Democratic Party's reaction to the Reagan phenomenon.

Unwilling to watch helplessly from the sidelines, Garvey entered politics shortly after and ended up suffering two humbling and bruising defeats: to arch-conservative Republican Senator Bob Kasten in 1986 (50.9 percent to 47.4 percent) and then to popular Republican incumbent Tommy Thompson in the 1998 gubernatorial contest (60 percent to 39 percent).

He also finished third in the 1988 Democratic primary for the open U.S. Senate seat created by the retirement of William Proxmire. But Garvey said he knew going in that he couldn't compete with millionaire Herb Kohl's huge war chest and stood little chance.

I'd interviewed Garvey twice during that period. In 1990, over the phone, for a profile I was doing of Kasten, and in the midst of the 1998 gubernatorial race, with his running mate Barbara Lawton, at the old Ovens of Brittany restaurant near Garvey's Shorewood Hills home.

As he reminisced about those defeats in 2011, it was clear that, while he opposed practically everything Thompson stood for, he considered Tommy a shrewd politician who had done some positive things as governor and felt no animosity toward him. But he was still seething about his defeat to Kasten—which came as little surprise to me. When I'd asked him in 1990 to describe Kasten in one word, he didn't hesitate: "amoral."

●

ZALESKI: I know the Kasten loss, in particular, was a bitter pill to swallow. Did either one have long-term repercussions?

GARVEY: Personally? No. First off, the loss to Thompson . . . several Democrats had come to me in 1997 and said, "Ed, you've got to run against Tommy because nobody else will. And if nobody else does, Tommy can use his huge treasure chest to help support [conservative Republican] Mark Neumann against [incumbent Democrat] Russ Feingold in his senate race." They told me, "If you run, you'll keep Tommy's feet to the fire, and therefore, Feingold and [liberal Democratic Representative] Tammy Baldwin can run their own campaigns and do well." So we talked about it at some length.

I mean, I'm not as dumb as I look. I understood that with the kind of money Tommy had and knowing what I'd be facing in trying to raise money, that winning was a *very* long shot. And, frankly, the only day that I thought we might actually do it was the first day of the campaign, because the *Chicago Tribune* had a big headline about corruption in Mayor Daley's administration, and the *Milwaukee Journal-Sentinel* had a big front-page story about corruption in the Thompson adminis-tration. And I thought, You know, it's just possible that people will say, "This is enough!" But, of course, they didn't. I mean, I don't know what you'd have to do to turn off the amount of money and the TV spots and all the other things Tommy had going for him.

But no, losing to Tommy wasn't much of a blow—it was more like a blip on the screen. But in terms of personal reaction, losing to Kasten made me angry for a couple reasons. One, he's the guy who beat the best senator this state's ever had—Gaylord Nelson [in 1980]. I thought, it's not a big deal if he beats me, but he's the guy who robbed us of Gaylord. This is not a good guy.

And two, he beat me with a lie. It was the beginning of the Roger Ailes success story, when Ailes [then chairman of the national Republican Party] went around the country running these dirty campaigns. And when Kasten said during the cam-paign that there was $750,000 missing from the NLF players' pension fund and insinuated that I had something to do with it, I was so infuriated I didn't know what to do. I thought, this will kill him, because when the press gets word of this and realizes there isn't a nickel missing, they'll skewer him!

Well, instead, I had the *Milwaukee Sentinel*'s Ken Lamke ask me, "Well, how much is missing?" There's nothing missing, jackass! What are you talking about? So we had Gene Upshaw and Ken Bowman and some other guys from the players union come out here to campaign and open the books—but nobody would come and look at them. And Kasten wouldn't talk to the press, so he just got away with it.

ZALESKI: It obviously still makes your blood boil.

GARVEY: Well, what concerned me about it was that I may have left Wisconsin worse off than if I hadn't run, because he *did* get away with that kind of stuff. It wasn't just a question of the not-so-good things I'd done in my life that they might put on a TV screen; it was if they don't have anything, they'll just make it up! And if they make it up and it goes on TV, people begin to think it's true, because they don't understand that . . . the National Association of Broadcasters made a deal with Congress that they'd put any TV campaign spot on provided that they'd be exempt from libel. And Congress said, "Ok, you're exempt."

The Kasten thing still angers me because we were ahead in the polls and then he used this terrible, untrue attack ad, and we dropped like a stone. Am I still bitter? Bitter's not the right word, but I decided back then that I was going to spend the rest of my life doing something about campaign finance reform. Because we couldn't respond to the Kasten ad in part because we'd spent all our campaign money. And the TV stations wouldn't take an IOU.

ZALESKI: As it is, Kasten outspent you by a considerable margin.

GARVEY: Yeah, I think it was like three to one. But you know, in the case of that $750,000 that the Kasten people claimed was missing, we wanted to go on the air and say, "Here's Gene Upshaw, here's Ken Bowman, here's Pat Richter. Not a dime is missing—this is an outrage!" But we didn't have the money to cut a new commercial. So we filed a libel suit, and it had the desired effect—we started climbing back up in the polls. And according to some Republicans later, we caught them on the final day of the election, but it wasn't quite enough to put us over the top.

ZALESKI: Where did the $750,000 figure come from?

GARVEY: From a book [*The Rise and Decline of the NFL*] written by Joan Baez's [then] husband [David Harris]. He wrote the book with Pete Rozelle, and he said that somebody had

Actor Ed Asner campaigns for Ed in his 1986 U.S. Senate bid against incumbent Robert Kasten. Garvey was ahead in the polls until Kasten's campaign ran a TV ad alleging Garvey had stolen money from the NFLPA's pension fund. Garvey lost the election but later won a libel suit against his opponent. (Garvey family photo)

told him that it was unclear from reading reports about our pension fund where some of the money went and that Ed Garvey couldn't answer the question. Well, when this came out, I had Gene Upshaw and Ken Bowman and Tom Condon and others from the NFLPA fly to Wisconsin to say it was all bullshit! Take a look at the books!

But the Kasten people took a quote from that book that Garvey didn't have any answers about where the pension money went. And we said, "Well, there hasn't been a nickel missing from any fund during the time that I'd been head of the union. Never! You're crazy!" But it worked. We dropped fourteen points in the polls, we sued him for libel, and suddenly

I started going up again and, as I said, essentially caught Kasten in the polls by Election Day. But the information came from this book, which this guy wrote with Rozelle. We figured Rozelle and the owners wanted me in the Senate like I want Parkinson's disease. So anything they could do to help anybody who would bring me down, they'd cooperate with. That's the only thing that made any sense.

ZALESKI: I'm guessing it took a while to recover from that whole ugly campaign?

GARVEY: It did—and it certainly didn't help that I needed to get a job right away. I mean, people don't factor in that when you run for office as a Democrat or Progressive or whichever, it's not just about raising money. It's the fact that you have to give up making a living. So unless you were very careful in selecting your parents, all of a sudden you've got to find a job.

Now, I had the notion at the time that most of the big law firms in Wisconsin would want me in their office because everybody in the state knew who I was. Just the opposite— because the type of clients who'd go with the big law firms didn't want anything to do with somebody with my political beliefs. So Betty and I had to think about what we were going to do next.

ZALESKI: So that's what led you to start your own law firm in Madison, specializing in environmental cases?

GARVEY: Yeah, pretty much.

ZALESKI: Did you take any time off to recover from that defeat?

GARVEY: Yeah, we went to Mexico—Puerto Vallarta. I thought I was in heaven. We were there about a week. But I got over the loss fairly quickly—I mean, what are you going to do? You can't wallow in it. So you just have to make plans and move forward.

ZALESKI: How about the defeat to Thompson in 1998— were you emotionally drained after that one, too?

GARVEY: No. I think maybe the funniest moment of my political life occurred that night. We had dinner here at the house with the Lawton and Garvey families before going to the so-called victory party at the Great Dane restaurant downtown. And at 8:01 p.m. public radio could hardly contain themselves, saying Thompson had won. So we all go down to the Great Dane, and the black delegation that was the core of my campaign in Milwaukee said, "C'mon Ed, we've got to talk to you before you say anything to the press." So I said, ok. So we go off into this corner, and this guy says, "You've got to get up in front of those cameras and announce you're running for mayor of Milwaukee. You'll get 95 percent of the black vote, and you can fool half the whites, so you're a shoe-in to get elected."

ZALESKI: He was serious?

GARVEY: Yeah, he was serious! And, of course, I was laughing so hard at that point, I thought, if I get up there and say I'm running for mayor of Milwaukee, my wife will hit me from twenty paces with a beer mug. But we never had a moment of any seriousness that night. Everybody had a good time.

Bill Kraus, the local political pundit, wrote a commentary about the two victory parties that night. He said he went to the Garvey party and everybody was having a great time. Then he went to the Thompson party, and it was like somebody had shot Tommy's dog. Because Tommy wanted to prove in that race that he could carry minority votes, the city of Milwaukee, and women—and he lost all three.

ZALESKI: Despite a massive advantage in campaign spending.

GARVEY: Right. He had as much money as he wanted. I think he outspent us ten to one, something like that. I mean, how do you beat that? It would be like running against Herb Kohl. You can't just write out a check for $1 million any time you feel like it.

Civil rights activist and former presidential candidate Jesse Jackson (*center*, with Garvey and running mate Barbara Lawton) at a rally during Garvey's failed 1998 gubernatorial bid against incumbent Tommy Thompson. (*Milwaukee Journal-Sentinel* archives)

ZALESKI: Did you ever regret running against Tommy?

GARVEY: No, because it had the desired result. We were able to raise a lot of important issues, so Tommy and the Republicans had to stay focused on the race. So Feingold was reelected to the U.S. Senate, and Tammy [Baldwin] was reelected to the House. So I thought it was all worthwhile. I think Betty did, too.

ZALESKI: Does Betty share your lingering anger over the Kasten debacle?

GARVEY: I think so. Our whole family was upset with the fact that I settled with Kasten before we could go to trial, because they wanted our day in court. Jim Doyle was my lawyer—this was four years before he was elected governor. And he said, "You really have to settle because a jury's probably only going to award you a dollar—because it's politics and most jurors don't care about what's said in a political campaign."

But I did do some second-guessing on whether I should have settled with Kasten or taken him on. The lawsuit had Kasten and Roger Ailes as defendants, so just taking the depositions would have been fun. "Now here's Roger Ailes of Fox News." God, what a beauty he is.

ZALESKI: Nonetheless, you still believe settling out of court was the right decision?

GARVEY: Oh, I think it was, because I think the danger is you spend way too much time being the Monday morning quarterback—looking back and saying, "What could you have done?" And I just had a better feeling about looking forward and seeing if we could do something to build a better Democratic Party in Wisconsin and do something about campaign reform. I figured that the world could continue to spin on its axis if I was not in the U.S. Senate, and that I could probably do more good outside of the Senate than spending the next six years trying to figure out how to get back there.

ZALESKI: Reflecting on those defeats, is there anything you could have done differently that might have changed the outcomes?

GARVEY: Not really. The only second guessing against Kasten was whether I should have done more to make sure that the vote came in properly. We had suspicions that Kasten's people were holding back votes in the northwestern part of the state, because the votes just weren't coming in on election night at the rate they should have. And the results seemed skewed.

ZALESKI: Any particular lesson you learned from those setbacks?

GARVEY: Money, money, money. If we can't control the money in political campaigns, then you're kidding yourself if you think you have a democracy. It's just foolishness. Yes, somebody who's outspent *can* win. But so what? Most people who are outspent cannot win or do not win. Because, as Senator Tom Harken [Democrat-Iowa] says, you can probably survive if you're outspent two to one, but beyond that, forget it. Miracles happen, but not very often.

ZALESKI: Do you think the general public grasps that yet—that vast sums of special-interest money have tainted the entire electoral process and have made it almost impossible for average Americans to run for higher office?

GARVEY: Yes, I think so. And the only reason I say that is because when I'm giving speeches to college students or progressive groups, you do get this sense that they get it, that they know what the game is. Now, do most people care? That might be the more important question.

Actually, another lesson comes to mind from my U.S. Senate race. We were in Wausau one night, the last stop after campaigning all day. My staff said, "You've got to go to this bowling alley." And I said, "A bowling alley? Where people have been drinking all night and it's after 10:00—are you kidding?" So we walk in and these four guys are standing there, and one says, "What do you want?" I said, "I'm Ed Garvey, and I'm running for the U.S. Senate." And this guy says, "I suppose you're a supporter of that God damn Gaylord Nelson." And I said, "Yeah, I am. I love Gaylord." And he said, "Well, you can thank him for the Hmong that are over here now."

And I said, "No, you can actually thank Nixon for that"—because of the Vietnam War and so on. So he says, "Well, I find you to be ridiculous, so you ought to get out of here because we're having a good time." And I said, "Look, we're taking a campaign survey—can I put you down as undecided?" And his bowling mates practically fell on the floor laughing.

One of them said, "Ed, we're going to vote for you. Don't worry about this guy—he's nuts." And we left.

But my advice to anyone who's running for office—don't go where there's alcohol being served after 10:00 at night. You're just walking into trouble.

12

ENVIRONMENTAL TRIUMPHS

For all the attention afforded Garvey's NFLPA tenure and his hard-fought but ultimately disappointing political career, I've always felt his most significant achievements came in environmental matters. In particular, the inspiring leadership role his law firm played in protecting Wisconsin's air and water from out-of-state corporate invaders.

As a columnist, I wrote about environmental issues on a semiregular basis. That included, of course, the three grassroots victories that the state's environmental community, with the unwavering support of Garvey and his partner Glenn Stoddard, somehow pulled off: blocking Exxon from building a copper and zinc mine near the pristine headwaters of the Wolf River in northern Wisconsin; thwarting Perrier Inc. from locating a giant $35 million bottling plant in Adams County—a plant that would have endangered vulnerable natural springs near Wisconsin Dells; and stopping New Mexico–based Holsum Inc. from building a factory farm in rural Rock County, about five miles east of Evansville.

Even more amazing, those triumphs were attained without the support of the Wisconsin Public Intervenor Office, which Governor Tommy Thompson and his fellow Republicans had dismantled in the mid-1990s. Created by the state legislature in 1967, the intervenor office defended public rights in the waters and other natural resources in Wisconsin. It even had the ability to sue to stop pollution or protect drinking water.

Garvey readily agreed that those victories were the high-water marks of his legal career. His eyes twinkled when I brought them up, and he was delighted to provide some additional context and details as we resumed our chats on a gray, damp April morning.

●

Zaleski: We've talked about the political setbacks you've endured, but I'm guessing those were more than offset by your law firm's role in some monumental grassroots environmental victories the last two decades. Looking back now, how significant were they—and is there anything progressives can draw from those efforts today?

Garvey: Well, I think they were very significant because it was sort of the beginning of a grassroots movement in Wisconsin to protect the environment, family farms, and the health and safety of citizens.

But those battles were different in the sense that we didn't have the constraints of the Democratic Party telling us what we could or couldn't do. We just did what we thought would make sense, so we organized people, got signatures.

I remember in the Perrier case, we had our first meeting in the late 1990s with the town folk in Adams County, and a guy from Perrier was there, and he said, "We want to be good corporate citizens. So if you don't want us here, we'll leave." And almost everybody said, "Good, then leave." And he said, "Well, I don't think this is a representative group. We need a bigger meeting."

So they organized a bigger meeting, and beforehand Perrier distributed leaflets and more people showed up. And he said, once again, "We want to be good corporate citizens—if you don't want us here, we'll leave." And pretty much everybody said, "Leave!" Then he said, "We don't think this is a representative group either. We need a referendum." So we said, "Fine, we'll have a referendum."

So we had the referendum. Seventy-six percent of the voters opposed Perrier. Then a member of the village council noted that 24 percent of the people favored Perrier, and he said he was going to support the project on their behalf.

So we had a recall election and recalled the guy with almost the same percentage of the vote that opposed Perrier in the referendum. That's when Perrier decided to pick up and move to Michigan. And the taste of that victory was so satisfying that that's when we formed Fighting Bob Fest.

ZALESKI: Perrier was the impetus for Fighting Bob Fest?

GARVEY: Yeah. A bunch of us got together at a Perkins restaurant in Wisconsin Dells and asked ourselves, "What should we do at this point?" And the conclusion was, we needed to have—for lack of a better term—a strike force where if citizens in a village or town wanted to stop someone from, say, building an ethanol plant near a school, we could send people in to help the locals shape the issues, look at the alternatives, see if there's any legal recourse, recruit people for boycotts, and so on. And that's when we came up with the idea to have an annual meeting—which we decided to call Fighting Bob Fest, after former Wisconsin governor and senator Bob La Follette, the greatest progressive this country has known.

The idea was that the environmentalists from across the state who get involved in these movements get to know one another and develop some sense of camaraderie. Then, if somebody calls—as they did in the Town of Porter in Rock County— and said, "Hey, they're trying to put a factory farm in here," we could send people in to help the locals stop it.

ZALESKI: The Town of Porter's ability to stop the factory farm in 2000 was downright startling—and inspiring. As I recall, locals didn't have much hope in the beginning of that battle.

GARVEY: Yeah, that was interesting because this corporation wanted to put in a huge factory farm—I think it was 2,800 cows—and Tommy Thompson's ag department and his tourism people were in favor of it. And after a series of volatile meetings, the five-member village board voted on it. The vote actually took place in the school gymnasium because the crowd that showed up was too big for the town hall. As you can imagine, it was a very dramatic moment.

The first board member said, "I think factory farms make sense but not here, I'm voting no." The next one said, "I've listened to all the arguments so on, I'm voting no." Now all we needed was one more, and I'm thinking, "Oh my God, we can't lose now—or can we?" And the third member sort of dangled it out there for a few minutes and then said, "I'm voting no"—and the place erupted with applause and cheers and hugs.

ZALESKI: A gratifying moment, to be sure.

GARVEY: Absolutely. And again, it was a victory of these local citizens and small farm people who could stop a multinational from coming in and taking their land and their water and their air . . . and I think it gave people across Wisconsin the sense that they *could* do things like that.

But I think it's important to point out that the success in all these cases was in a nonpartisan context—not in a Democratic Party context. The Democratic Party, one had the feeling, paid no attention whatsoever to what we were doing. It wasn't even relevant to whatever the hell they think about. Perrier, the factory farm in the town of Porter, the Crandon mine . . . those were all cases of progressives operating together.

ZALESKI: If you had to cite one crucial factor in those long-shot victories, what would it be?

GARVEY: We told people the truth. We never lied to anybody. "We" being the committee of citizens—probably twenty in the beginning who were opposing Perrier.

We met at a gymnasium in the Dells, and that sort of became the catalyst because the local assemblyman essentially said to us, "You should all just get used to this because Perrier is going to get permission. They're going to build this plant, so stop fighting because it's going to create jobs."

And we said, "Listen buddy, your job is to represent us, and we don't want it here. We don't want the trout streams and the wetlands dried up, and we don't want the traffic, the blacktop, and all the rest of it."

And he basically said, you're going to have to learn to live with it. "Well," we said, "we're not." And it just took off from there.

ZALESKI: A turning point—Perrier's opponents weren't backing down?

GARVEY: Yeah. We had all these hearings, and people began to realize what was happening and that Perrier wasn't being honest about the impact this thing would have on the ground-water. And as more and more people got up to express their opposition, we just got this feeling, "We can beat them!"

And when we stopped Perrier, I had the feeling that we were beginning to develop a commitment to the environment that was meaningful—where we could bring in resources other than money and scare the bejesus out of the local assemblyman or state senator or the mayor or the village board president and say, "Hey folks, this is important to us, get out of the way!"

So I think those battles were terribly important in terms of the confidence factor. But it never spilled over into the Democratic Party. And the Democratic Party never spilled over into those battles.

ZALESKI: And I don't think the average person realizes how bleak those situations seemed at the beginning, in both situations. Same thing with the proposed Crandon mine in northeastern Wisconsin, which was finally defeated in 2005.

I remember interviewing an Exxon official at his Rhinelander office and how exasperated he was by the steely resolve of the mine's opponents. By all appearances, he complained, "The strategy here is to try to create as much noise and confusion around this thing as possible," adding that he'd never been involved in a project "that's as politically out of control as this one."

Is Wisconsin really different, as he suggested? In other words, is it our genes? Or would other states have stopped these projects as well?

GARVEY: I think to some extent it *is* in our genes. At least it seems like there's more of it here. Take something like Fighting Bob Fest. It's just kind of a picture of what happens in the state. When Bernie Sanders and Tom Harkin came here, one of the first things they said was, "Ed, we couldn't do this in Vermont or in Iowa."

I mean, I think there is a spirit of independent action here that's stronger than it is in almost any other place. I don't know why. I would attribute it mainly to the La Follette era, the progressives, and the great state University of Wisconsin—which

[Chancellor] "Bye Bye" Biddy Martin wants to turn into Private Citizens U. So I think it is different.

ZALESKI: As important as those triumphs were, they seem like ancient history today. Do you think most of those who showed up to protest Scott Walker's agenda at the state Capitol are even aware of them?

GARVEY: For the most part, no. The luster wears off after a while. So whenever a new battle comes along, you've got to start all over, recruit new people.

And the opposition, of course, has gained some knowledge as well. They're willing to put some money in and make some compromises that take some sting out of the proposal.

ZALESKI: Even so, I assume those victories rank among the highlights of your legal career?

GARVEY: Yeah, they do. Because, why do you become a lawyer? I mean, it's for social and economic justice. I've been lucky in that I've met a lot of great and inspiring people.

I mentioned earlier meeting Eleanor Roosevelt as a college student, and how she gave us a tour of Hyde Park and then gave us a little speech about how we have a duty to society to help the less fortunate and how she wanted to make sure we were fulfilling that responsibility.

You'd get the same advice from Gaylord Nelson or Hubert Humphrey or Henry Reuss. So you don't go into the practice of law so that you can make a lot of money.

ZALESKI: You're being facetious, right?

GARVEY: [Smiles.] Ok, many lawyers *do* go into it to make money. But that's not why I wanted to become a lawyer. I wanted to be a lawyer so I could help citizens do the kinds of things that we did.

ZALESKI: I doubt even your harshest critic would question your motivation for becoming a lawyer. At the same time, I'm sure they'd also point out you've done quite well financially.

You do, after all, live in a gorgeous, seven-bedroom home in upscale Shorewood Hills.

GARVEY: Well, I've never said that we've suffered. But no one can suggest that I got as much money out of the things I've done that I could have if that had been the primary objective.

I mean, when our firm took on the tobacco case in the 1990s, where the three law firms that helped Wisconsin sue big tobacco claimed their time was worth $847 million, nobody else wanted anything to do with it. But we won.

And after we won, a reporter asked me, "What did you get paid out of it?" Well, we got nothing—we paid money *into* it! We picked up the cost of prosecuting the case. But you still feel good about it.

I mean, this is what lawyers are supposed to do—in my view. And as I think about what's been happening in the state of Wisconsin over the last decade or so, it takes some leadership to get average people involved in these causes. Because the general response to a problem like Perrier or the legal fees for the tobacco lawyers or whatever, is that you can't beat city hall. So you've got to get people involved who say, "Yes you can! And here's how you do it. Here's how we did it with Perrier and in the Town of Porter."

ZALESKI: Well, it may have worked in the past, but environmentalists are hardly encouraged by what they've seen from Scott Walker so far. And many believe it's only going to get worse.

GARVEY: Right. What's happening now with the DNR and the governor and so forth is that the full weight of state government comes down on the side of these big companies, and it's much more difficult and costly for citizens groups to fight them.

So things have not gone well for average citizens in Wisconsin the last couple years, and it's just a lot more difficult to get people riled up because they look at it and think, we can't stop it. So it's kind of scary.

ZALESKI: Many environmentalists would say that Thompson's decision in 1995 to dismantle the Wisconsin Public Intervenor Office was the first major blow in this battle. In his victorious campaign for governor in 2002, Democrat Jim Doyle vowed to restore the intervenor office, but—to the dismay of environmentalists—it never happened.

GARVEY: Yeah—that and public financing of political campaigns. Doyle never even tried on the public intervenor, and he certainly didn't do anything about campaign finance reform either.

ZALESKI: Do you think we'll ever see the day when Wisconsin has a public intervenor again?

GARVEY: No—not unless we change the system. There aren't any Democrats who are even campaigning on that issue anymore.

ZALESKI: And the reason?

GARVEY: Because it's too controversial. If you're the public intervenor, you're taking on corporate powers. For instance, if Exxon's proposing to build a mine, the public intervenor's job is to make sure the DNR does not let Exxon create the mine without following all the rules. That's why all the developers, the highway people, and others hated the public intervenor office—because it could stop a project for years.

So if a Democrat ran for office today and supported bringing back the public intervenor, big business would say, "If you're for the public intervenor, don't come around here for money." So it all gets back to money.

And Republicans will say the reason there's high unemployment is because of these out-of-control environmentalists. Businesses won't come to Wisconsin because the regulations are so strict it's damn near Russia—that's what DNR stands for. And while that sentiment was always there in the past, it's so much larger now.

ZALESKI: We've talked about your great admiration for Gaylord Nelson. Could an environmental crusader like him be elected to the U.S. Senate today—or win the presidency?

GARVEY: Why of course—isn't Ralph Nader president? Oh that's right—he barely got 3 percent of the vote.

13

The Anti-Environmentalists

Garvey felt so intensely about the need to protect the environment that he asked that we continue the discussion at our next session, just a few weeks after Earth Day. He was perplexed that an issue that once appealed to Democrats and Republicans alike no longer resonated with the leaders of either party—but especially Republicans.

As we discussed this disturbing reality, I was reminded of an interview I did in 2004 with Fred Risser, a Madison Democrat who was first elected to the state senate in 1962. In those days, Risser noted, there were at least a half-dozen Republicans who regularly voted to protect the state's air and water. What's more, Republican Warren Knowles, who served as governor from 1965 to 1971, was a staunch environmentalist. Now, Risser lamented, there was only one Republican senator—Robert Cowles of Green Bay—who would be considered pro-environment. And even then, not on every issue.

Risser was dismayed—and deeply saddened—by this development. Wisconsin is renowned for its sparkling clean lakes and streams and had long been an environmental leader. In

1970 it was the second state to ban DDT, just ten months after Michigan had. (The Environmental Protection Agency issued a national ban in 1972, an action that led to the eventual recovery of the bald eagle, which was removed from the endangered species list in 2008.) Were Republicans—and more than a few Democrats—really willing to relinquish our precious natural resources to the highest bidders?

To Garvey, it was a textbook example of how big-money special interests—obsessed with their bottom lines—had corrupted our political system and muddied the public discourse. And, in so doing, had pointed the country down a dangerous path with little regard for future generations.

●

ZALESKI: Protecting the environment certainly would qualify as one of those contentious issues that Democratic leaders often ignore—which is perplexing in light of all the polls that show a vast majority of Americans place a high value on clean air and water. Some Democrats even refrain from talking about global warming, for fear of being attacked by conservatives. And many remain silent when Republicans talk about eliminating the Environmental Protection Agency. Nelson must be spinning in his grave.

GARVEY: Well, you're right, and it's almost inexplicable when you think about Nelson and Earth Day, and Aldo Leopold and John Muir, and all the others who dedicated their lives to environmental issues. And when you think that Wisconsin was the only state that once had a public intervenor office, it's pretty hard to believe what's happened.

I mean, this used to be Wisconsin's hallmark. Not just clean elections, but clean air and clean water. Then we got this huge infusion of money into politics, so every issue today somehow circles around money and gets you from behind.

The first question is always, how much money can you raise? So if you're Jim Doyle and you're governor, it's how much money can you get from the utilities? And should you happen to raise tens of thousands of dollars from the utilities, does anyone in the Democratic Party question whether the utilities might have an agenda? Well, you'd have to be insane to think they don't. They're not giving away money because they think you're Mother Teresa.

My friend Bill Kraus was saying the other day there are now something like thirty-four thousand lobbyists in Washington. I mean, that's a staggering figure. And when you have former Democratic leaders like Dick Gephardt and Tom Daschle and others now working as lobbyists—you ask yourself, why is that? Is it because Dick Gephardt is an expert on anything? No. It's because he was such an important person in Congress. And if he gets money to support clean coal and gives it to somebody who's running for office in Wisconsin, people say, "Well, it comes from Dick Gephardt, so it has to be ok." And that's what these corporations are buying—the reputations of the people who are involved in politics. So, until you get campaign finance reform, you're not going to get back to the idea of protecting the environment. It's pretty pathetic.

ZALESKI: In 2007, top scientists from around the world signed a statement declaring, in essence, that not only is global warming real but it's driven by human activity and is already wreaking havoc in certain parts of the planet. And yet, Democrats rarely speak out when some conservatives say it's all a hoax. How do you explain it?

GARVEY: It is hard to figure. I mean it's like we're living in a dream world, for Christ's sake. We know that the storms today are more severe, the hurricanes and tornadoes are getting stronger—all the predictors are that if we don't do anything about the environment we're going to die. And even then, you can't get people to do anything. Why? Because some claim we can't afford to do anything—who's going to pay for it? It's just so outrageous it's hard to believe.

I look at my grandkids and think, what the hell am I leaving for them? "Uh, listen kids, the next fifty years are going to be rough. But you can handle it. I'm sure there will be some innovations that will clean up all that stuff."

ZALESKI: And as environmentalists point out, there's little downside to switching to alternative fuels since we have to do it anyway because fossil fuels are becoming more scarce. It's just common sense, isn't it?

GARVEY: Well, you have be nuts to think that global warming isn't happening. You look at the pictures that some of these photographers have been taking in the Arctic and Greenland and so on, and you see what's happening—you see the icebergs melting and the tons of ice being deposited in the sea.

We know what it's going to do in terms of raising the sea level—over time, it's going to eliminate certain countries in the world. It could eliminate New York City and all of Florida. And you mention that to some people, and they'll nod or smile and then it's, "Yeah, but who are the Cubs playing today?" or "What about abortion?" Abortion? How about saving the planet!

ZALESKI: But give the Republicans and the big oil companies credit—they've pretty much succeeded in confusing the public on environmental issues. It's always, "These environmental regulations are strangling big business."

GARVEY: Oh, no question. You watch some of the TV spots— they'll have a tall, stately woman waltzing toward the camera saying, "Do you realize the oil industry provides seven million jobs?" Or you'll see a Chevron ad that claims we've got all the oil we need—it's just locked in these rocks and all we have to do is get it free from these rocks and we'll have more oil than we need for the thirty, forty years, whatever.

Completely crazy! We know it's polluting all the streams and rivers and the air that we breathe, but the oil companies are out spending billions of dollars to buy up all this land in the Southwest so they can frack the oil out of there, which is even more difficult than getting the gas out. And then it gets into the water supply.

ZALESKI: One does wonder what it's going to take. Many people have already forgotten the disastrous BP oil spill in the Gulf of Mexico, which happened just two years ago, and favor expanding oil drilling in the gulf. I'm guessing you're not surprised?

GARVEY: Well, Gore Vidal has referred to this country as the United States of Amnesia, because it seems to suffer a bout of amnesia every three months or so. For some reason, we lack this ability to reflect on past events—unless it's sports related.

ZALESKI: A recent *New York Times* story noted that there are tens of thousands of chemicals already on the market, but that fewer than 10 percent are ever tested for their effects on human health. It's astounding, isn't it, that nobody really knows whether these products are causing cancer or not? Some wonder if this is the smoking gun—the reason behind this country's off-the-charts cancer rates, the autism epidemic, or the alarming increase in Alzheimer's and Parkinson's diseases, among others.

GARVEY: Come on, don't be so negative! You don't think companies would put their products out there if they thought there might be a problem with them, do you? What the hell's the matter with you? Cynicism has grabbed your soul!

No, you're right, something clearly is going on. You don't have to be a scientist to say, "Look, in the last twenty years or so, we've had this epidemic of autism, this epidemic of Alzheimer's, this epidemic of Parkinson's, and so on." It's just incredible. So, what's changed? I mean, something's obviously changed.

My dad used to smoke, started when he was fourteen. Two packs of Pall Malls every day. Didn't quit till he was eighty. I said, "Dad, why are you quitting?" And he said, "Well, it's not good for you." And I said, "Dad, I've got some bad news for you. This is a little late." And he replied, "It's never too late to quit! And they don't taste good anymore either." And that's when I knew he was really dying, because he didn't want any whiskey either. [Smiles.] I thought, something's wrong here.

He died shortly after—of pneumonia. But my point is, in those days people just didn't get cancer. Now, if my dad could smoke two packs of cigarettes a day and live to be eighty, with little adverse impact on his health, there was something different about the environment than there is today. I mean, today, it's just a matter of what type of cancer you're going to get.

ZALESKI: If you were ten years younger and decided to run for the U.S. Senate again, what environmental issues would you raise?

GARVEY: Well, you'd have to start by giving the power to the EPA to really regulate greenhouse emissions. Because if you can't do that, we're not going to save the planet. You'd have to talk about climate change and the impact it's having on weather and the economy and the future of our country.

But it's tragic—there's almost nothing happening now in regards to protecting the environment. Look at Wisconsin. People have asked me, "What would you do about this proposed huge iron mine near Ashland in northern Wisconsin?"

Well, if I were running for office now I'd say you've got to stop it. This isn't a Third World country that's going to be left scarred.

I just read Bobby Kennedy Jr.'s new book, *The Last Mountain*. I never knew about the topping of the mountains that's going on in West Virginia and other states until he spoke about it at Fighting Bob Fest. It just blows my mind that you could have a company come in and say "We're going to knock off the tops of these mountains, and the sludge is going to run down and jeopardize the rivers and the people down below"—and people would stand for it.

Or all the new undersea drilling that's been proposed in the Gulf of Mexico. We've got to stop this nonsense or we'll reach the point where the gulf can't be saved. And never mind if it annoys the oil companies.

ZALESKI: Some environmentalists say it's time to rethink nuclear energy. Where do you stand on that?

GARVEY: Well, if the recent catastrophe in Japan hasn't taken care of that issue, I can't imagine what would. I mean, for heaven's sake, Germany's going to eliminate all their nuclear plants in twenty years or something like that now. We've got to do the same thing.

But we do need to shift to alternative sources of renewable energy—wind power, solar, and others. Everything has to turn on a sort of a Marshall Plan to develop an independence from oil and coal. Otherwise we're doomed. We're at the point where we need to take drastic action.

14

PERILS OF OVERPOPULATION

After exiting politics and turning his focus to environmental issues, Gaylord Nelson spent the last decade of his life giving speeches about the perils of overpopulation. And not just the population explosions in India and China or in impoverished nations in the Mideast and Africa—where, in many cases, the problem of too many mouths to feed is exacerbated by severe drought and other impacts of global warming. He worried about the rapidly growing population in the United States— which, he pointed out to anyone who would listen, in just a few short decades would dramatically affect our quality of life. And yet, politicians from both political parties ignored those warnings or, in some cases, refused to even acknowledge them—mainly, Nelson maintained, because the issue was too explosive to discuss in public forums.

In fact, the Sierra Club—to cite just one example—once considered overpopulation its number one concern. Nowadays, it tries to avoid the issue out of fear it will inflame members on both sides: conservatives, who are horrified by any talk of limiting births, as advocated by Dr. Paul Ehrlich in his

contentious 1969 book, *The Population Bomb*—which, out-
landish as it seems now, the Sierra Club had copublished; and
its liberal members, who refuse to even consider reducing the
flow of Latin American and Mexican immigrants, lest they be
labeled racists.

Having written about overpopulation several times during
my career and coming to share Nelson's belief that it is *the*
most critical issue facing humankind, I was curious how Garvey
felt about the subject. To my surprise, he seemed as worried
about it as Nelson was and welcomed the opportunity to explain why.

●

ZALESKI: Gaylord Nelson agreed that there were credible
arguments on both sides of the overpopulation issue, but that
we should at least have the conversation. We owed it, he said,
to our grandkids and great-grandkids.

GARVEY: Well, look what's happened just the last two years
with abortion. It's just astounding. In some states, they're now
talking about putting doctors in prison for performing abortions. I thought that this was all settled law, way back when
Roe v. Wade was decided [in 1973]. In fact, I remember thinking, "Thank God, we're finished with that issue. Now we can
talk about poverty and low-income premature birth and things
like that."

But no, we're right back at it. Everything is, "How do we
stop abortions?" I mean, it's just nuts. In many ways, it's worse
than it was before *Roe v. Wade*.

ZALESKI: The *New York Times* recently reported that the
United Nations is now predicting that the world's population
will swell to 10.1 billion by 2050. The United States, meanwhile,
will add another 156 million by 2050, boosting our population
to 478 million. Nelson said that in this country it's really a

quality of life issue; if our population continues to swell, what will the quality of life be like for our grandkids—and their kids? [Editor's note: Although birth rates are now declining worldwide—including in the United States—the planet's population is still expected to hit 9.8 billion in 2050 and 11.2 billion in 2100, according to a 2017 United Nations report. That's partly because, the report said, people are living longer. The United States' population is projected to reach 400 million in 2050.]

GARVEY: Yeah, I remember when Gaylord used to say, "Imagine what Wisconsin will be like if our population doubles. Imagine the effect it will have in terms of lost farmland and the increase in the number of roads, prisons, and so on." But nobody wants to talk about it.

ZALESKI: He was especially worried about the impact on our natural resources—the strains on our water supply, for instance.

GARVEY: But again, it's this inability or refusal or failure of our educational system to face reality. There's almost no discussion about real issues anymore. If you look at Scott Walker's budget that's going to pass the legislature, he's cut almost $1 billion out of our public schools over the course of the next two years. What the hell happens to these kids? I mean, do we not know that a lack of education leads to other problems—like the need for more prisons—or are we just totally stupid?

ZALESKI: Nelson's biggest frustration, again, was that nobody even wants to talk about it—and that we're fast running out of time to find solutions. He'd say, "Let's at least have the debate."

GARVEY: Right. But just think about the Catholic politicians—or conservative, Christian-right types. You think they're about to touch this issue? Just think of the people who are running for president on the Republican side. Would any one of them be pro-choice? I don't think so. [Mitt] Romney was for a while—although Ted Kennedy had a great line. He said Romney was actually multiple choice.

It just seems like we can't have a debate about any issue, because somebody's going to get hurt or mad and they'll cut off funding. Or you're going to have a Tea Party uprising.

People keep saying to me, "Things have got to get a lot worse before they can get better." Well, who do they have to get worse for? And how do you stop it once you go down that path?

ZALESKI: It's always the poor and working-class families that are most affected.

GARVEY: Of course. I remember when I first heard that over 50 percent of black adult males in Milwaukee were unemployed. Mike McCabe [then executive director of the Wisconsin Democracy Campaign] told me that. And I said, "My God, that must be exaggerated." Well, I checked it out—and it's true!

During the Great Depression we never reached 50 percent unemployment that I know of. But when you have 50 percent of a population that's unemployed, you're going to have problems! But what you get now, instead of a debate, is a race to see who can come up with the biggest cuts in W-2 and the rest of it.

So none of these critical issues are discussed because they're too hot. Part of it's money, and part of it's that the politicians are afraid that the public won't go along with it.

ZALESKI: The reason we need to confront the issue now, Nelson would say, is because it's not one of these problems where we can just slam on the brakes. If we wait another decade or so, it'll be too late. Was he being an alarmist? Or, from your perspective, is it a legitimate concern?

GARVEY: Absolutely, it's a legitimate issue. And to not discuss it is as silly as not talking about climate change. I mean, there are certain forces that are occurring in our universe that if you don't talk about them, you certainly can't deal with the problems that are being created.

When Obama was down in Joplin, Missouri, recently, after the horrible tornado down there, he never even suggested that climate change was causing the kinds of things that happened in that city. He said, "We're going to be with you, we're going to march with you, we're going rebuild with you—and let's start now. Somebody hand me that board over there. Let me start by cleaning this up." No answers, just sympathy.

Or take Hurricane Katrina. If you look back at that disaster, there should have at least been a discussion afterward about whether it even makes sense to rebuild New Orleans—where the sea level is rising and the city sits in a bowl. I mean, what's going to happen here next time?

But there was no discussion—only things like, "Oh, let's just blame Bush for not acting quickly, for not doing his job." And Bush, of course, doesn't have the courage to say, "Well, wait a second folks, maybe we shouldn't even be doing this because the city's just going to be wiped out by the next major hurricane."

I mean, what's going to happen if the sea level down there goes up just three or four feet because of global warming? Can you imagine how much money they're going to ask the federal government for to try to save that city? Or how about New York? Or Miami? Or Charleston, South Carolina? The costs will be enormous. And then people will say, "Why didn't you warn us about this, for God's sake?"

So yeah, it's very scary. If you can't recognize the problems that you have, then you certainly can't come up with any cures or solutions. Years ago, if you had an epidemic like polio, the scientific community responded and worked like hell and found a way to defeat it. But nobody today is taking that attitude toward overpopulation, toward climate change, or toward education. I can't think of any major issue that we're dealing with in an adult fashion.

ZALESKI: Does that suggest a failing of the media?

GARVEY: Oh, forget the media. They've totally dropped the ball. But how about the universities? How about Florida State University, which has essentially sold its econ department to the Koch brothers? And here in Wisconsin we've got [Chancellor] Biddy Martin wanting to privatize the University of Wisconsin–Madison, so you'd have the utilities and other corporations essentially running the place and deciding who's going to be on the faculty and deciding who gets a degree and who doesn't. I mean, why aren't Wisconsin residents just screaming about this? Privatizing the UW–Madison campus? Are you out of your mind?

ZALESKI: So how do you explain that type of attitude? Is it ignorance? Apathy? Human nature?

GARVEY: All of that, I suppose. I remember my mother gave me a book when I was a kid called *You Can Change the World*, written by a priest known as Father Jim [Keller]. And in one chapter he mentioned being in Kokomo, Indiana, one day and how he was talking about the problems in India and Pakistan and Brazil and the southern part of the United States. And then somebody came up to him at the end of his speech and said, "But Father, things are all right in Kokomo."

And that was his next chapter, "Everything's All Right in Kokomo." And I've often thought about that—hey, everything's all right in my little community. Everything's fine in Shorewood Hills. Problems? What are you talking about?

15

DEATH OF JOHN MACKEY

Two days before our next session, John Mackey, a Hall of Fame tight end for the old Baltimore Colts and the first president of the NFLPA, died of dementia-related symptoms. He was sixty-nine. Although Mackey had been suffering from the disease for years, I knew he and Garvey had been close and that the news would be a major blow for Ed.

I didn't realize just how much until Garvey met me at the door with a pained look and apologized beforehand if he didn't quite seem himself that morning. But after a few sips of coffee, he began reminiscing about the brother-like bond he'd had with Mackey, and that infectious Garvey smile—and wit—soon returned.

To older football fans, John Mackey was one of the premier players on the Colts teams of the 1960s that were one of the Green Bay Packers' fiercest rivals. Fast, tough as nails, and a punishing blocker, Mackey teamed with quarterback Johnny Unitas and halfback Lenny Moore to give the Colts one of the most explosive offenses in NFL history.

But it was as NFLPA president that Mackey—a brilliant, shrewd, unshakable tactician and negotiator—had his greatest impact. And it's largely due to his efforts—along with Garvey, of course, and other player reps of that era—that today's players enjoy a standard of living that NFL old-timers never even imagined.

While he clearly was shaken by Mackey's death, Garvey said he was even more distressed by his friend's slow, heartbreaking decline. It caused him to question what a violent, brutal game football is and to wonder aloud whether it will still be around—indeed, whether it deserved be around—twenty years from now.

ZALESKI: It's no secret that John Mackey suffered from dementia in recent years, but I can see his death still hit you hard. How would you describe your relationship with him?

GARVEY: John Mackey was a central figure to everything that happened to me with the NFLPA—we wouldn't have a union if John Mackey had decided to go to Slippery Rock University instead of Syracuse. What I mean is, John was the son of a preacher who insisted that he go to a school that would give him a four-year scholarship no matter what—whether he got injured or not. Syracuse offered that, so he went to Syracuse.

He understood that what was needed for athletes was to have some security. He used to talk about the NFL as a machine, and how they have parts factories all over the country. So if a tight end loses a knee, they can call in another tight end from Detroit or someplace else and patch it in. But I also think John fully appreciated the fact that he was going to have a good education no matter what happened.

ZALESKI: You mentioned earlier that Mackey wanted you to represent the players union back in 1970 and that he wouldn't take no for answer. How did he hear about you?

GARVEY: Are you kidding? Everybody had heard of Ed Garvey. [Smiles.] What happened was that the NFL and the old AFL got congressional approval to merge in 1966–67, but the actual merger occurred in 1970. So the first season with different teams and leagues and so on was that year; the two unions came together and decided to merge, consolidate, whatever you want to call it.

The AFL Players Association was run by Jack Kemp, who was a company fink from day one. And the NFL Players Association was run by the more militant players—Ken Bowman, Pat Richter, Eddie Meador, and some others. So the first thing they had to do when they merged was to elect a new negotiating committee and a president. So they elected Mackey president of the new union.

So Mackey meets with the union's executive committee, which was made up of Bowman and Richter, Kermit Alexander, Tom Keating, Nick Buoniconti, and a couple others. And he said to Richter and Bowman, "Hey, you guys are in law school at the University of Wisconsin. Ask your labor professor [Nate Feinsinger] who we should hire as labor counsel." They said fine.

So they go see Feinsinger, who had recommended that I go up to Minneapolis to Lindquist and Vennum because it was the best labor firm around. Feinsinger told them, "I sent Ed Garvey up to this firm in Minneapolis. I think you ought to go with them or a firm in Milwaukee. But you might be a little hesitant to go with that firm because they represent Jimmy Hoffa and the Teamsters." And to be honest, the players did get kind of crazy at that prospect.

So my firm got a letter in the mail asking, "Would you be interested in being the labor counsel with this newly formed organization called the National Football League Players Association?" I mean, here we were in Minneapolis, it's twenty-below zero, and would we like to represent the NFLPA? We all started joking, "I'll take the Miami games. You get San Francisco . . ."

ZALESKI: You were elated, in other words.

GARVEY: Oh yeah. So John Mackey flew to Minneapolis with Alan Miller, and he and John sat down with Leonard Lindquist and myself and a couple other lawyers from my firm, and we agreed to represent them. Then we notified the NFL that we were going to represent them—and with that, Rozelle tried to convince Mackey that he shouldn't hire outside attorneys because attorneys just bring big egos and lots of problems.

The league had its own lawyer, Alan Miller, and Rozelle asked John why the union needed to bring in an outsider. And John said, "Because I feel more comfortable with somebody else. So Pete, you take care of your business and I'll take care of mine."

ZALESKI: What was it that set Mackey apart from others?

GARVEY: Well, first off, John was an extremely bright guy, a wonderful storyteller and a good speaker. He was a leader extraordinaire who could really convince the group to do just about anything because they had such respect for him as an athlete, as well as for his intelligence.

But when we got started in collective bargaining, John just wasn't going to take any nonsense from the NFL. They thought they could just roll over the union and force them to accept a long-term agreement, and John just made sure that wasn't going to happen.

ZALESKI: Did it take much arm-twisting?

Garvey: It did, actually. When he asked me to do it, we'd just gone through the 1970 negotiations, and I said, "Hell no." He said "Why not?" And I said, "Betty and I just bought a house in Minneapolis, I'm finally with a law firm, I'm enjoying the work, and I want to get involved in politics." I told him, "I love representing you guys but I don't want to do it full time." So he said, "But Ed, it's part of the civil rights movement, you have to do it." And I said, "Well, I don't think so John."

So about a week later, he called me and said, "What did Betty say?" I said, "About what?" He said, "You know about what—quitting the law firm and coming to work for us." I said, "I haven't raised it with her." And he said, "I'm flying to Minneapolis tomorrow. We're going to get this done."

So he came to Minneapolis and convinced Betty and me that we should do it for a short period of time—get the union started so they could take on the NFL effectively. I remember Betty turning to me and saying, "Don't get old too quick—why not do it for a couple years and see how it goes?"

So Mackey was delighted. But I did tell him I'd take the job only under one condition—that it was approved by a unanimous vote of the executive board. John said ok—and sure enough the vote was unanimous. And that's how it came to be. But what John understood was that the players had to be organized if they were going to take on the NFL effectively. And the only way to do that was to hire someone like me to be executive director and put together a staff and the necessary funds that you'd need. So we just started from scratch and went from there.

Zaleski: You endured a lot of flak during your twelve years with union—and almost overnight became one of the most hated sports figures in America. Did you ever regret your decision?

GARVEY: Oh, I had my moments. But John was right—
it *was* part of the civil rights movement. I mean, one of the
most important parts of John's presidency—and for those
who followed—was to force the NFL to integrate, to hire black
coaches and to give black players the same opportunity on the
field as white players. So his contribution was significant.

ZALESKI: Recent polls show that a majority of Americans
actually favor unions and their right to collective bargaining.
But I'm guessing most people—including a fair number of
liberals—still think it's ludicrous and grossly unfair that athletes are paid millions of dollars for, as the saying goes, playing
games for a living. You heard that a lot when you first took the
job, obviously, but that sentiment is still out there.

GARVEY: Right. But I used to say to people, "Tell you what.
If you'll put on the pads and the uniform and play in the National Football League for a couple of weeks, you'll find out
why they're getting paid these kinds of salaries."

But yeah, we knew when we formed the union that there'd
be a lot of those who said, "What are you doing worrying
about players who are making all that money when migrant
workers are barely getting by?" And our response was, "It's
not necessarily that kind of choice." I mean, you can represent
the players and get them fair compensation—and also work
for Cesar Chavez or the machinists union or whatever.

The other thing John and I believed was that if you laid it
out for most people and said, "Look, here's your choice. Should
the money should go to [team owners] George Halas and Carroll Rosenbloom? Or should it go to the players who actually
play the game?" And they'd side with the players every time. I
mean, every time Lou Harris took a survey, the fans supported
the players two to one over the owners.

What was distorting everything, of course, was that virtually all the big-name sports columnists in the country—
guys like Dick Young, Dave Brady, Bill Wallace, and Dave

Anderson—were anti-player, pro-management. And so they gave the impression that the players were just prima donnas who were seeking more money than they deserved and constantly telling everybody that the fans supported the NFL owners. Which just wasn't true.

ZALESKI: How would you describe your personal relationship with Mackey?

GARVEY: I doubt if I've ever been closer to anyone in my life—other than Betty, of course. He was a special friend.

ZALESKI: He was still living in Baltimore when he died. Were you still communicating with him regularly?

GARVEY: Well, for the last five years he was totally out of it, so no. The last time we saw him was about seven years ago in Minneapolis, when my old law firm flew him in for Leonard Lindquist's ninetieth birthday. John gave me a big hug and asked, "Who are you?" Same thing with Betty. It was very sad. I mean, here was a good friend, a great leader, who'd just lost it.

ZALESKI: Do you think his dementia was related to the injuries he suffered during his football career? As you know, there's growing concern that playing football for a living could be detrimental to one's health—especially their mental well-being.

GARVEY: I have no idea, but you'd have to be silly to rule it out. Whether one could make the direct link or not, I think the answer is probably yes. In fact, if I were the NFL commissioner right now, I'd be spending enormous sums of money trying to figure out how to protect the players from head injuries—instead of saying we should have two more regular season games. Or let's take another look at the helmets.

I mean, for heaven's sake, if the evidence seems to be that these repetitive hits to the head are linked to dementia . . . unless you deal with that and deal with it immediately, the game could come to an end. It could be like boxing at the University of Wisconsin. When Charlie Mohr got killed the ring [in 1960], university officials essentially said, "Well, that's enough of that." And they banned the sport shortly after that.

ZALESKI: The *New York Times* seems to be out in front on this—they've written a number of stories in recent months about the ramification of all these brain injuries to former NFL players. And some believe it starts with concussions suffered in high school football. Unless they figure out a way to prevent those injuries, you might see a growing number of parents encouraging their kids to play other sports instead.

GARVEY: Absolutely. And I think it's happening already. I know a lot of NFL players who told me they'd never let their kids play football—in Pop Warner leagues and so forth.

ZALESKI: But it's not just the NFL that, until recently, has tried to minimize the potential ramifications. Football's become so popular that many fans would prefer not to know that many former players are suffering from brain injuries. They don't want anyone tampering with their game—injuries or no injuries.

GARVEY: Right, just like they don't want to hear how artificial turf has caused more injuries. They don't want to hear anything negative—and they love the violent hitting.

ZALESKI: And then someone like John Mackey dies—one of the all-time greats—and they're forced to think about those things, at least for a few moments. But the John Mackey you came to know was far from just a talented football player, obviously. How do you explain the chemistry you had with him?

GARVEY: Part of it *was* civil rights. I mean, when John graduated from Syracuse in 1963, the NFL was pure white in the coaching ranks and the front office. And blacks weren't allowed to play quarterback, middle linebacker, guard, or center—the cognitive positions.

So we *were* involved in the civil rights movement. I don't want to overstate that here but it was a part of the discussion. And we had some interesting moments. I remember when we went to picket the Baltimore Orioles' opening game the year that Clinton was elected president [1992]—his first year in office. Jesse Jackson had called and said, "Let's go picket to call attention to the fact that Major League Baseball, the NFL, the NBA, do not hire blacks, Hispanics, or women for off-field positions."

So we went to the Orioles game, and afterward the *Baltimore Sun* invited us to appear before their editorial board. And they couldn't believe that we would picket the Orioles because they had black players. And we said, "What does that got to do with it? We're talking about black players but also in off-field positions as well." And Mannie Jackson was with us— he'd played basketball at Illinois with Jesse Jackson and later bought the Harlem Globetrotters.

And the position of commissioner of Major League Baseball was open at the time. So Jesse said to these editors, "Here's just one example. The baseball commissioner's position is open—what are the odds they'll hire a black person?" And they said, "Well, do you know any blacks who'd be qualified to hold that position?" Jesse said, "How about Mannie Jackson, sitting right here." And they all laughed. It wasn't raucous laughter, but it was clearly a snicker.

And Jesse said, "What are you laughing about?" And somebody said, "Who said he's qualified?" And Jesse said, "Here's a guy who was vice president of Honeywell, who turned the Globetrotter franchise around, was an All-American at Illinois, and broke the color line at that school. And you're saying he's not qualified? Then tell me who *is* qualified."

16

Fighting Bob Fest

So if it's not hopeless, as Garvey insisted repeatedly in our sessions, how do progressives find a way to turn things around—much like Fighting Bob La Follette did at the turn of the twentieth century?

Garvey didn't suggest it would be easy, in light of how cunning, audacious, and powerful corporate America has become—as evidenced by its ability, with a significant boost from Fox News and other conservative media, to persuade average Americans to vote against their own economic interests.

But he did provide a blueprint of sorts, one he sincerely believed—with the right kind of leadership and if promoted effectively—could tap into the anger and resentment many middle- and low-income Americans felt and unleash a grass-roots uprising unlike any other. (I'm sure he was aghast that Donald Trump, of all people, somehow managed to exploit that resentment in 2016. And I'm guessing he was just as disgusted with his fellow Democrats for allowing Trump to hoodwink what was once a key constituency.)

As always, I admired Garvey's unbridled optimism and his unshakable belief that, in the end, good will prevail. But I admitted to him I was skeptical of that notion, which led to some of the most spirited exchanges we had.

●

ZALESKI: You've said all along that this year's Fighting Bob Fest—the event's tenth anniversary, held last weekend in the Dane County Coliseum—could be the most crucial one of all because of what's happened in Madison this year. What's the verdict?

GARVEY: I'm very pleased. Needless to say, we were worried that by moving the event from Baraboo to Madison, some people who celebrated with us in the past might not show up, or that people in general were just tired of the protests that went on here. But the enthusiasm people had for the speakers and the message that was delivered just restored the faith of all the people I was involved with, like Bernie Sanders, Cornel West, and Tony Schultz. I mean, this was a phenomenal lineup of speakers. And they got to the people who were there—none of the speeches were over people's heads. The people were excited, and the speakers were excited.

Bernie's the best speaker in the country, I think. And what a guy! And Jim Hightower alone is worth the price of admission. He's been a very important figure in the progressive movement. He goes everywhere, speaks to every crowd. They love him, and his message is always one of hope—never despair. I mean, you might occasionally catch him in a down moment over what's been going on, but for the most part he just thinks we don't have the right to have that luxury of beating ourselves up.

ZALESKI: I heard one estimate that about 6,500 people

Ed and fellow progressive Bernie Sanders in 2013. They were good friends for more than a decade. (David Giffey photo)

showed up—which led some Bob Fest regulars to suggest that estimates of 10,000 at previous Bob Fests in Baraboo may have been inflated. True?

GARVEY: I think the attendance this time was closer to 8,000—or even 8,500. We were trying to add it all up, but it was hard because some of the floors at the Coliseum don't have turnstiles. But I probably did overstate the crowd numbers in Baraboo somewhat. Whatever the numbers were, the feeling of fear I had as I stood on that podium for my opening remarks—looking out at all those empty seats—eventually went away. As the day went on, all those seats on the first and second levels were filled. So it was a darn good crowd, and a happy crowd. They loved it.

The biggest mistake we made was having the beer concession on the third floor. People had to walk up three flights to get a beer—and most people weren't about to do that.

But, you know, estimating crowds is always one of those things that's very difficult. The fire commissioner says it's 5,000, the police commissioner says it's 10,000, and the organizers of the event say it's 50,000. [Smiles.] Who the hell knows?

ZALESKI: So moving the event to Madison was a positive move?

GARVEY: Yeah, because it allowed us to focus on all the little details. When we held it at the Baraboo fairgrounds, we had to scrub down the stands, build the stage, all of this stuff, with volunteers. It was always a helluva lot of work. And when we'd have the kickoff on Friday night at the Barrymore Theater [on Madison's east side], the people who were doing all the work in Baraboo couldn't make it because they were working till dusk setting things up. So this way, everything is set up, there's plenty of room for the breakout sessions for the attendees—everything was good. So I think it was a good move.

ZALESKI: But, as in past years, the crowd had a decidedly gray hue to it.

GARVEY: Oh, I hope so. Because that's when I know I'm among friends.

ZALESKI: But we've discussed how critical it is for young people to be part of this movement. Have you changed your mind about that?

GARVEY: No, I think it's terribly important for young people to be involved. One of the reasons we moved Fighting Bob Fest to Madison was to get closer to the UW, thinking this would attract more students. But free parking and good speakers apparently isn't enough. I mean, I think there were more young people this time than in previous Bob Fests. I think every single person who attended the first one was gray-haired.

ZALESKI: Nonetheless, I'm guessing about 80 percent of those who were at the Coliseum last Saturday were over fifty. And I don't think I saw more than a dozen college-age students.

GARVEY: I agree. But, again, we deliberately moved the event to the second week in September so that we'd have some more time to talk to and recruit UW students. And then we offered free parking, and bus service was very accessible. But no, we didn't attract as many students as we thought we would, that's for sure.

ZALESKI: The fact that it was 60 degrees and sunny probably didn't help either. Not the kind of day you want to be indoors.

GARVEY: Right, beautiful fall day, Willy Street Festival, all of those things. But, you know, another way to measure the success of this thing is how much money people gave—and they gave $67,000.

Now that's amazing. I couldn't believe it when I saw those figures. Because I figured that we needed about $17,000 to break even. And the buckets alone that we passed around contained $31,000.

ZALESKI: That's impressive. But does the makeup of the crowd suggest that for this movement to gather steam and move forward, it will have to rely mainly on Baby Boomers— aging rebels from the Vietnam War days? At least for now?

GARVEY: Well, I'd like to find the answer to the question of how you motivate young people to get involved in politics. They're so turned off by the system, the Citizens United ruling, the Koch brothers, the buying of members of Congress—when they see what goes on with the lobbyists in Washington and Madison.

I think the cynicism runs so strong that it's hard to break through it. If we can get them to hear Cornel West or Bernie Sanders, we'll pick up a lot of them. I think the demonstrations at the Capitol attracted a lot of support from young people because it was exciting, something important was going on. But two weeks after it was over, [local progressive activist] Ben Manski tried to have a rally up there. He said to me, "Ed, where is everybody?" And I told him, "Ben, I've got news for you. If you think you helped create that [earlier] crowd of 150,000, you're delusional. Nobody knows how it happened, in my view."

But it happened. Something sparked it. And it became fun and the thing to do and the place to be. That hasn't happened again—and I don't know if it ever will. So what you have to do, from my perspective, is to say, "Listen, we need more blacks, we need more Hispanics, we need more women, we need more young people. In the meantime, I'm just going to go ahead with what we've got now—whether it's old white guys or old white women—till we get more people involved. Because that's what we have to deal with."

You can't lose the whole show because you're missing part of the cast. Do I regret it? Yeah, sure. Somebody always says to me after Bob Fest, "We didn't have enough blacks." Really? Well, no kidding! Cornel West, how about him? We make up in substance what we lack in the numbers, it seems to me.

I mean, I don't know what triggers these things. If it hadn't been for the sit-ins during my junior year at the UW, I wouldn't have become involved in civil rights. But something grabbed me when I saw how those people were being treated. When we brought a busload of students up from Fisk University to speak to the UW student senate, that grabbed me.

And I'm talking to these young people and asking, "How do you do this?" And they're telling me, "Well, you just sit in, and sometimes an angry white guy will come up and put a cigarette out on your girlfriend's back"—and I'm thinking, "Whoa! Say what? And you just have to take it? This isn't the sort of thing you'd see in my neighborhood." That changed my life.

ZALESKI: From that moment on?

GARVEY: Correct. So maybe some young person coming to Bob Fest and hearing Cornel West, Bernie Sanders, Ellen Bravo, or Tony Schultz is going to change their lives. I mean, whenever I give a speech, I look out at the audience and think, there may be one person here who will change their life because of this speech. But it may actually be ten, or maybe twenty. At Bob Fest, it may be two or three thousand.

I know they're going to be impacted, but exactly how much? I don't know. How will they show that they've been impacted? Again, I don't know. Will they take that step if there aren't demonstrations against the bankers or the war in Afghanistan or whatever? Time will tell. But we have to keep the flame lit.

ZALESKI: One of the smartest moves Obama made was to utilize social media—notably Facebook and Twitter—to reach younger voters. What are your thoughts on that? Is it something you might try to emulate?

GARVEY: I'm sure we have to do that. But I think Obama got young people involved mainly because he was a dynamic figure in the flesh. I mean, they stood in line when he spoke at the UW because they couldn't wait to see him, and you can't accomplish that through any kind of mechanical equipment.

My point is, I think they trusted him. The system's broken, and this guy says he's going to bring about change—and by God, I'm going to trust him to do it! I think that's why there's such a loud sigh among young people when you bring up Obama's name today. He just hasn't delivered. Now there've been recent signs that he's finally starting to stand up to [John] Boehner and all these other right-wing Republicans leaders, but it's been a long time coming. We'll just have to wait and see.

ZALESKI: There wasn't much media coverage of this year's Bob Fest—local or otherwise. I know you've complained about being ignored in the past.

GARVEY: No, not much. Channel 15 was there. And Wisconsin Public TV streamed it. Two radio stations, WOJB and WORT carried it live. And, the Thom Hartmann show had us on. The difference between now and, say, five or ten years ago, is that I can have a half-hour interview with Thom Hartmann and thousands of people are going to learn about Bob Fest. Or I can go on the Ed Schultz show. I mean, there's as much more coverage today from the noncorporate media than we've ever had before.

And I keep telling people, "Look, if we have 100,000 people who regularly visit our website, fightingbob.com, we can go around the corporate media. So what the hell difference does it make if the *Milwaukee Journal-Sentinel* covers Bob Fest?" They don't cover much out of Milwaukee anyway. I mean, most of the editors there wouldn't know how to get to Madison if you tied them to your steering wheel.

Otherwise, we always used to get a nice article in the Baraboo newspaper—I don't know if we got one this year. And the *Wisconsin State Journal* had a piece the day after the event that wasn't too bad. But the *Milwaukee Journal-Sentinel* has never bothered with us.

ZALESKI: You mentioned earlier that this movement has to be bigger than one individual—whether it's reelecting Obama or trying to recall Scott Walker. Would you elaborate on that?

GARVEY: Well, I've always maintained that presidential elections are the biggest enemy for organizers that you can imagine. Because they suck out all the energy—people are all-in for Jimmy Carter, Al Gore, Barack Obama, or whomever. And it's exciting and they can go to the rallies and the TV cameras are there. And just by being there they become part of the deal, and the balloons are dropped from the ceiling and there's confetti all over the place and everybody's having a good time and singing "Happy Days Are Here Again." So, yeah, it's exciting. But there's nothing much exciting about a gubernatorial race. Or a U.S. Senate race.

But Democrats look at Walker and say, he's the problem. And if we'd just beaten Republican Luther Olson in that [4th district] recall election, we'd have a Democratic majority in the state senate.

Well, I look at that election and say, "First off, somebody [in the Democratic Party] should have been vetting those candidates and said to [4th Dist. Democratic candidate] Fred Clark, 'Sorry, but you're out for a couple of reasons.'" But if you're looking at it from just that perspective, what would have changed had Fred defeated Luther Olson? The Democrats would have a one-vote majority in the senate. But all you'd need is for one of those Democratic senators to sell out, and they'd lose their advantage anyway!

So when you look at recalling Walker, I just say to people, "Look, there's every reason in the world to recall him. But the question is, who do you have warming up in the bullpen?" In other words, let's say Walker *is* recalled. What happens next? Who runs against him—and can that person win? Mike McCabe [former executive director of Wisconsin Democracy Campaign] determined that $44 million was spent on the senate recall elections: $44 million! At a time when labor is now without automatic dues checkoff on paychecks. So AFSCME [American Federation of State, County, and Municipal Employees] and WEAC [Wisconsin Education Association Council] are no longer able to pour millions of dollars into these races.

And there's going to be a split between those who say, "Well, it's going to be more important to defeat Walker" and those who say, "No, we've got to elect more Democrats to the

Mike McCabe, former head of the Wisconsin Democracy Campaign, chuckles at a Garvey one-liner while waiting to speak at the 2012 Fighting Bob Fest. (David Giffey photo)

legislature to try to get our public funding back so that public schools can survive. And we just don't have that bottomless pit of money." So it seems to me that all the hoopla about the need to recall Scott Walker—well, sure I'd like to. And you never know what will happen with this FBI investigation of Walker's staff.

But everything else being equal, if you have a recall election for Walker and you don't win, you've really caused a problem. Because there isn't any money left for any other candidates. I mean, we're confronted with a [Republican Party] juggernaut here that has a bottomless pit of money. So I just think very little thought has been given to how the Democratic Party is going to react to and deal with the Supreme Court's Citizens United decision.

If they can't deal with that, I'm not sure what can happen. You've got to have the ground troops ready to get out there and make sure enough people vote—people who are so angry that you can actually beat the Koch brothers. But if we try to play the Koch brothers' game, we lose.

ZALESKI: So you're suggesting that if the Democrats don't succeed in recalling Walker, they could end up even being more demoralized?

GARVEY: I don't think demoralized, but they could up more in the hole financially. And more and more potential candidates are going to say, "I'm not going to run."

ZALESKI: You said you were extremely disappointed that Feingold ruled out running against Walker. Why?

GARVEY: Because I think Russ could overcome any of the money that the Koch brothers could throw in.

ZALESKI: So he's without question the best candidate the Democrats could put up against Walker?

GARVEY: Oh yeah. Sure.

ZALESKI: Is there anyone else who stands a chance? I know there's talk of former Congressman David Obey running. Are there any young, shining stars standing in the shadows?

GARVEY: Not many. Or if they're there, the shadows are very dark.

ZALESKI: If this is the beginning of a new progressive movement, how important is it for the Democratic Party leadership to get on board—both statewide and nationally?

GARVEY: I don't see the Democratic Party playing any role because they don't want the Bernie Sanders of the world to thrive—or even survive.

ZALESKI: Because of their ties to big money?

GARVEY: Right. There's only one party today—with two branches. And they're both after the same sources of money:

The insurance industry, the pharmaceuticals, oil, and gas. You go down the list and they're all there.

ZALESKI: So the only way this movement ignites is if it's grassroots?

GARVEY: Has to come from the bottom up—has to.

ZALESKI: So the blueprint, as you see it, is to expand the number of Bob Fests each year and, at the same time, start organizing to get progressives elected to positions of power in villages, towns, and cities throughout Wisconsin? And then hope that the movement catches fire nationally?

GARVEY: I don't see any other way to do it.

ZALESKI: One of the biggest obstacles, which you alluded to earlier, is persuading good people to run, knowing that the Republican right will try to drag their name through the mud. We've reached a point, sad to say, where a lot of good people don't want any part of it—so we're left with mostly zealots and zanies running for higher office.

GARVEY: Exactly. Twenty years ago, we would have said, "This is ridiculous, stop it!" If Dwight Eisenhower were president and this stuff was going on in the Republican Party, he'd say, "Hold on here, time out. We've gotta have some rules." Now, it's all been turned over to the Lee Atwaters and the Karl Roves.

These are mean, nasty people who think winning is the only thing that matters. And the Democrats have their brand as well. So you approach somebody about running for higher office today and, well, it's very difficult to say the least.

I remember when I tried to get Alan Page [former Minnesota Viking star, now a justice in the Minnesota Supreme Court] to run for the U.S. Senate after Senator Paul Wellstone died in that plane crash. He said, "Ed, I thought you were my friend." What do you mean? "Are you crazy? Why would I do that?

I'm on the Minnesota Supreme Court, things are quite nice. I have a nice family, get to see the grandkids all the time. And you want me to give that up to do what? Tell me again, slowly." And I think this is the part of the calculus that people don't tend to focus on.

ZALESKI: An incredibly sad commentary.

GARVEY: When I came back to Wisconsin and got involved in politics, I figured all you had to do was get organized, get people involved, get people excited about the issues, lay it all out, write a book—whatever it might be. Get your ideas out there and attract people to it. Have a sense of humor. Work as hard as [former Wisconsin Senator William] Proxmire. And you can win!

I thought, this will be a piece of cake because I'll work harder than Bob Kasten, and he's a bad guy and he beat the greatest senator we've had in my lifetime. And besides that, Kasten had his own problems. Then suddenly there was $750,000 supposedly missing from the players' fund, and the Kasten people say Garvey doesn't know where it went.

It's pathetic because of the personal toll it takes. My kids, for example . . . when Kasten came out with those TV commercials that I'd essentially stolen this money, Kathleen was at the UW, and she said to me one night, "I don't know what to say anymore, because people ask me, 'Well how much *did* he take?' Not, is it true? But, how much did he get?" After that election, when I'd give speeches around the state, I'd say, "Actually, I did steal the money and we're living off the interest. That's why I can afford to give this speech for nothing." I mean, you might as well laugh about it. But for most people, that's not laughable. It turned my kids off to politics completely.

ZALESKI: But weathering personal attacks is one thing. Trying to defeat candidates who now have access to unlimited campaign funds—thanks to Citizens United—is another.

Proud father Ed at daughter Kathleen's wedding in 1996. She is married to Joe McNeil. (Barry Lewis photo)

GARVEY: That's the crisis as I see it. The Mark Pocans, the Tammy Baldwins, the Jerry Browns—these people have to just grin and bear it and get out and try to raise money. And having done it in 1986 . . . I often joke about how I'd say to a friend, "Can you give me some money?" And he'd give me $1,000, and I'd say, "What, you had a bad year or something? How about $5,000?"

My mother and father told me from the time I was old enough to understand anything that the Garveys don't take, we give—that you're down on this earth to do good and not to take money from other people. And running for office requires just the opposite of everything you were taught as a child. Everything's counterintuitive.

Feingold, I think, has to be saying to himself, "One more loss and you're done." And he knows the Republicans could put in $30 million or $40 million against him if he ran for re-election to the U.S. Senate—easily. And now some people actually know who Ron Johnson is.

So I think Feingold must have also concluded that it wouldn't exactly be a cakewalk if he ran for governor against Walker. I don't know this for a fact—Russ doesn't confide in me and never has. But I think a factor he must have considered is that he lost his senate seat to a guy nobody knew—to a guy who looks like he belongs in the wax museum. And yet, this guy won! So maybe he did run a lousy campaign and his campaign manager was off the beam or whatever—nonetheless, he lost to a nonentity—by over 100,000 votes! And nothing's changed to make anybody believe those votes are going to switch back. So I think as Russ looks at the landscape these days, he's got to be mulling over the same things we've been talking about here.

ZALESKI: Makes sense.

GARVEY: A few years back, I attended a conference in Gulf-port, Mississippi, that was sponsored by Phil Stern—who wrote *The Best Candidate Your Money Can Buy*—and the Center for Responsible Politics. There were about forty or fifty people at this conference. And when I was called on, I went up to the board and wrote down $6 million. I said, "Ok, folks, let's have a little exercise office here. Six million dollars is what you need to run for the U.S. Senate to have a chance to win. Where do we get it if you're a progressive Democrat?"

Someone says, labor. "Ok, let's say we get $250,000 from labor. Now all we need is $5.75 million." How about environmentalists? "Yeah, let's say $10,000 from environmental groups." How about senior citizens? "Right. Another $50 from senior citizens."

And this really grabbed Phil Stern. He said, "Jesus, this is powerful stuff, because nobody understands this. Because they all sort of think, 'Hey, if you're Democrat, you're going to get labor's money. Or you're going to get this money or that money.'" But the ugly truth is, you end up having to go to all the people and businesses you dislike—like the insurance industry and the pharmaceuticals—to get the big money.

Look what Obama's doing now—he's chasing around Wall Street. I mean, the reality here is that maybe Obama hasn't consciously let us down. It's that he knows that unless he goes for this money, he has no chance of winning. So he says, "I'm going to raise $1 billion." And I say, "My nose is six feet long. What are you talking about, you're going to raise $1 billion? You could buy a country for that." Well, I suppose you could buy Paraguay—that would be kind of nice. You could have your own army.

ZALESKI: There was a recent article in the *New York Times* about how California Governor Jerry Brown is having a tough time coming to terms with how much politics has changed—and how polarized politicians have become—since the last time he was governor, in the 1980s. The Republicans won't compromise on a single thing.

GARVEY: Right. And I think if Obey somehow were elected Wisconsin's governor, he'd find the same thing. It wasn't that long ago that the two parties got along fairly well—when there were lots of different Republicans who were halfway decent people. Now the vast majority are mean as hell. This is the part that's so discouraging—and drives me crazy.

ZALESKI: We've talked about how Bob La Follette overcame extraordinary odds in turning the country around in the early 1900s. But the circumstances were vastly different—for one, he had the media on his side. If La Follette were alive today, could he replicate what he did one hundred years ago—or has the country changed too much for that to happen?

Garvey: I think it can happen again. That's why I keep fighting. That's why I push every button I can. And maybe there's nothing behind some of those buttons. But maybe there's something behind a few of them. It could be a small victory in a remote state that leads to a bigger victory. It could be winning a critical election because the voters were fired up and turned out in large numbers because you found a particularly bright, sensitive, articulate candidate for an office. In the long run, we have to feel optimistic, because if you look back at our history, we've always somehow emerged stronger than we were before this.

Zaleski: We being?

Garvey: The country.

Zaleski: And you've witnessed a flicker of hope at these protests—which you cling to now?

Garvey: Absolutely. I walked around the square and said, "Wow, the Republicans have to be saying, 'By God, there goes the future. It's gone.'"

Zaleski: So the next step for Ed Garvey is to feed off of what you witnessed at the Capitol?

Garvey: Feed on that, feed on Bob Fest, and take it around the state—maybe even around the country. And have this kind of populist uprising. I mean, it can happen! It's just that we have to be damn smart about how we use our resources. Because in the old days, the first thing you did was try to get the maximum amount of money from labor—$1.5 million or whatever it might be, and then you were off and running. Well, you're not going to get that anymore. So we've got to figure out a different way to do it—maybe like Gaylord said about putting down the tin cup and say you're not going to accept any of this special interest money and go from there. And you'll lose at first, but eventually you'll start winning it all, because people understand that the system is corrupt. And they want candidates who are honest and who they can depend on. I mean, I think the majority of Americans went for Obama because they decided, here's an honest man. I think it's why they went for Gaylord and why they went for Jerry Brown again in California. And there are still some candidates out there who exude honesty and can make a difference.

ZALESKI: Sounds good in theory.

GARVEY: There are going to be some breakthroughs. We just have to keep giving people a chance. We've got to get those maybe fifty people whose lives were changed at Bob Fest a week ago—because they were fired up by Bernie Sanders or Cornel West or Ellen Bravo—and convince them to keep going. Or maybe they heard the amazing speech by Tony Schultz, a farmer from Marathon County, and said, "Hey, I can do what he's doing."

And that's the beauty of what's been happening in Madison this year. Ordinary citizens—fire fighters and police officers and nurses and teachers—understand now that they can have an impact and that they don't just have to sit back and take it. How exciting is that?

17

LIZZIE

In addition to suffering two grueling political defeats, Garvey experienced some wrenching personal challenges as well—challenges I don't think most people were aware of. His youngest daughter, Lizzie, now in her mid-forties, has severe autism. And, as I mentioned earlier, Ed was diagnosed with Parkinson's disease.

Lizzie was not, he would always emphasize, a burden. Difficult, at times, yes. But a burden? Never. To the contrary, he would say, she was a godsend.

●

ZALESKI: You've mentioned to me in the past how you relish having Lizzie sit beside you on your cart when you golf at Blackhawk Country Club—and how she always seems thrilled to be a part of that. But I'm sure you and Betty and your two other daughters have experienced some incredibly difficult moments as well.

It's not widely known, for instance, that the primary reason you left the NFLPA in 1983 and returned to Wisconsin was because this state has one of the finest autism programs in the country. Accepting the job as Wisconsin's deputy attorney general was a secondary factor, from what I understand.

GARVEY: That's correct. Several years after Lizzie was diagnosed with autism [in 1975], Lou Brown of the UW's Waisman Center spoke in Washington on the importance of mainstreaming developmentally disabled kids. As I recall, Betty came home that night and said, "We're moving to Wisconsin. They have this program called mainstreaming. . . . It could make a difference in Lizzie's life, and let's just go."

So there really wasn't any choice. And I was all for it. There aren't too many things more important than how you deal with an autistic child.

ZALESKI: How old was Lizzie when she was diagnosed?

GARVEY: Around two and a half. We had some concerns at the time and talked to her pediatrician, who said she had a hiatal hernia. If you laid her down, she spit everything up. He said we had to keep her propped up, but that it could slow her development a bit. So we just relied on that diagnosis. Then a neighbor suggested we seek a second opinion, which we did.

ZALESKI: What was it about her behavior that gave you concern?

GARVEY: She just wasn't the same as other kids her age. She was developing more slowly. But again, we thought the pediatrician was probably right, that it was just the hernia.

ZALESKI: This was about fifteen years before the beginning of the autism epidemic, wasn't it? Most people didn't even know what autism was back in the 1970s.

GARVEY: That's right. And we felt that in Montgomery County, where we lived, the attitude was that kids like this should be institutionalized—and not exactly forgotten, but that they'd be happier with their own kind. And we said, we don't think so.

Ed adored his daughter Lizzie, who has severe autism. When he golfed at Blackhawk Country Club, she often rode along in his cart. (Barry Lewis photo)

We went to the Kennedy Center in Georgetown, then to Johns Hopkins University Hospital, and then to an autism institute that I thought was a fraud and a total rip-off—anywhere we could to have someone tell us what was wrong with her and how we could make it right. So we tried just about everything and moving back to Wisconsin was a big part of that process.

ZALESKI: What was your reaction upon getting the diagnosis—beyond the shock of it? Anger? Fear?

GARVEY: Sadness. I'm not sure even the medical community used the term autism back then. I remember going home to tell my parents in Burlington. And right before that I was sitting with Kermit Alexander, the Rams' player rep, in a hotel in Chicago—we'd just had a players meeting. And I told him it was going to be tough for me to talk to my parents about this. And he said, "Don't be silly. Your parents love you and they'll love Lizzie and you'll be fine." And he was right. As it turned out, my parents had suspected something was wrong. But yeah, my first reaction was just profound sadness.

ZALESKI: How would you describe her disability?

GARVEY: Well, she's unable to speak. But she's a lovely child, and a very loving child. She can't talk, but she can look you in the eye and take your hand or just touch you . . . and your heart wants to break.

But she can be a real challenge, too. When she was twenty-six or twenty-seven—a little more than ten years ago—we took her up to Washington Island in Door County. And she was as naughty as she could possibly be. I mean, it was just a miserable trip. And it became clear that she did not want to be hanging around with parents anymore. So shortly after, we got a guardian ad litem appointed and found her a place to live—out near Channel 3 on the southwest side.

And after we dropped her off and said our goodbyes, Betty and I stopped for a bite to eat, and neither of us could say anything the entire dinner. It's hard enough to see a normal kid go off to college, graduate, or whatever. But leaving your autistic child in an entirely new environment was pretty tough. Fortunately, she settled in fine.

ZALESKI: The explosive increase in autism cases began in the early 1990s, and for a long time many parents of autistic kids—and more than a few medical experts—believed it was caused by vaccines. Today, that theory is widely debunked. What do you think is behind the epidemic?

GARVEY: Honest to God, I'm not smart enough to know. I don't think it's vaccines, but I also don't think it's just a case of the disease being misdiagnosed years ago. Like a lot of things today, I think it might be something in the atmosphere or the water we drink or whatever. I mean, why is it that when we were kids very few people got cancer? Now it seems like everybody's got cancer. We never even heard of autism in the 1950s and '60s, and now we hear about it all the time. I don't know, but I suspect the environmental factors are more of a factor than vaccines.

But whatever it is, they shouldn't stop looking. Because, you know, it might be vaccines—who really knows? It's sort of like Parkinson's disease, which also seems to be on the rise. You just don't know. I mean, what the hell's happened here? I didn't ask for this.

ZALESKI: The odds of having a child with autism have increased alarmingly in just the last few years . . . it's something like 1 in every 110 now.

GARVEY: Oh yeah, it's an enormous problem. And the costs of having an autistic child are staggering, where you have to have staffed homes and so forth. So when you get someone like [Representative] Paul Ryan saying, "Well, I've got a good idea, why don't we get rid of Medicare and everybody can just kind of take care of themselves. . . ." We couldn't get health insurance for Lizzie when we first got back to Wisconsin because the insurance companies said they don't take retarded people. That was their initial response. But we just continued to raise hell and finally got some insurance for her.

ZALESKI: I've read of parents with severely autistic kids who are bitter, not only over the unfairness of it all but at God— assuming there is one. You've never felt that way?

GARVEY: No. I've never been one of those who ask, why me? I figure God's got a lot of other things to worry about. Frankly, I've never understood that kind of thinking. You play the cards you're dealt with. That's just the way it works. You know, some kids are geniuses and go off to Stanford and other kids get autism or cystic fibrosis or some other disease and spend a lot of time in hospitals or getting treatment. Life's too short to be blaming somebody for what we don't understand.

ZALESKI: Still, it must have been a blow at first.

GARVEY: Well, of course it was upsetting. And I just have to say that Betty has been the rock through all this. She was always looking for improvement from Lizzie. She's the one who took care of her when she lived at home her first twenty-eight years and took her to school and so forth. She keeps track of who all the staff people are [at the Central Center in Madison, where Lizzie now lives], their backgrounds, what they're doing, Lizzie's medications, the doctors who are treating her—just making sure everything's being done right. I mean, she's been phenomenal.

ZALESKI: I know they were both young when Lizzie was diagnosed, but how did your other two daughters, Pam and Kathleen, react when they found out their baby sister was autistic?

GARVEY: They just took it in stride. I mean, what are you going to do? Get mad? Sock a punching bag? We'll even laugh about it in that sense. For instance, Kathleen will say, "Lizzie, we know you're the favorite, so don't try to deny it." They just love Lizzie very much.

But, you know, so much of life is a snapshot of a particular moment. Flash forward to 2011, and I'd have to say we've just gone through the toughest period of Lizzie's thirty-eight years. And I'm happy to say she's doing quite well right now. But she wasn't doing well earlier this year. She couldn't swallow, she was losing weight, she was unhappy. And we couldn't figure it out because she can't speak. There were even moments when we weren't sure we'd be able to keep her alive.

But the doctors at the Central Center really worked hard and finally figured out what was wrong. One thing that happened is that she must have fallen and broken some ribs. So the pain caused her to not want to eat and she wasn't able to sleep. You'd think this would be obvious, but it wasn't.

Anyway, the snapshot today is good, and she's here every Sunday for breakfast. That's my one contribution—I make breakfast for Lizzie every Sunday morning: fried eggs, pancakes, and cheese, all the stuff that's good for you.

ZALESKI: I admire your attitude—and that of your family. That's the key to dealing with something like that, isn't it?

GARVEY: I suppose. But I must say that overall we've encountered some of the most wonderful people you could ever meet in the disability community. And wonderful, remarkably talented staff people, most of whom have someone in their family who has some sort of disability. So we've always said Lizzie is a real blessing in that sense. I don't mean to get goofy here, but her illness has brought all sorts of good people into our lives.

ZALESKI: Do you think we'll see a cure for autism in Lizzie's lifetime?

GARVEY: Well, that's our hope, of course. Of all the inspiring things politicians have said over the years, the one I've liked most is Jesse Jackson's "Keep hope alive." So, yes, we continue to hope there will be a breakthrough. If that happens, we always kid around that Lizzie's first words will be, "Can't you guys take a joke?"

18

Battling Parkinson's

In the summer of 2008, shortly after I'd lost my columnist's job at *The Capital Times*, Garvey called and asked me to join him for a beer at the Main Depot tavern on Main Street, across the street from his law office. A longtime fan of the paper and an occasional contributor to its op-ed page, he was as befuddled as most readers by the paper's decision to lay off a significant part of its staff and end its daily print edition. He wanted to know how veteran staffers in particular were handling the news.

As one of those staffers, I was hardly pleased but naively assumed that, because of my nearly four decades in the news business, I'd easily find another journalism-related job. While that never happened—ageism and a collapsing economy, I quickly discovered, were a toxic combination—I was touched by Garvey's concern and words of encouragement. We weren't close, but he wanted me to know that he empathized with what I and other laid-off staffers were going through.

As I noted earlier, it was during that conversation that he mentioned, rather casually, that he'd recently had a startling setback of his own: he'd been diagnosed with Parkinson's disease and was still trying to sort out the implications of that jarring reality. So in our final interview in 2011—some three years after he'd first disclosed his diagnosis to me—he agreed to talk about the impact the disease was having on his life and how he wrestled with the angst it was causing his family. While he'd long since come to terms with the diagnosis, he clearly was frustrated by having to cope with his declining physical skills. But hey, he said more than once, what else can you do?

Which, I'd come to realize, was one of Garvey's secrets for coping with life's misfortunes in general: Why complain? It's wasted energy. Just deal with the cards you've been dealt . . . and move on.

●

ZALESKI: As challenging as Lizzie's situation has been, you've had to endure another personal setback the last three years—being diagnosed with Parkinson's. How's that going?

GARVEY: Well, I've thought about it and decided to hell with it—it's not a good thing. Actually, I'm doing quite well. You hear what's going to happen, or could happen, with this disease, but the thing about Parkinson's is that it's a slow-moving disease, so it's not like you die the next day or something. And the medication's been doing pretty well for me— that and exercise. I'm taking Zumba classes on Fridays and Tai Chi with Betty on Wednesdays and I walk on the treadmill every morning.

ZALESKI: What were the first symptoms?

GARVEY: The last two fingers on my left hand weren't functioning very well on my computer keyboard. There were times they'd hold down keys and I didn't even realize it. You know that maddening sound the laptop makes when you hold down a key too long—scares the crap out of you? That happened to me several times. So I went to the Dean Clinic and said, "What's going on—what is this?" They said it's like carpal tunnel syndrome—that I'd probably been overdoing the typing. Take four Ibuprofen and you'll be fine.

Well, I wasn't fine—it didn't get any better. So I went back and they sent me to a neurologist. And the neurologist said, "Guess what? You've got Parkinson's."

ZALESKI: That must have been a jolt.

GARVEY: It was a surprise, certainly. I wasn't thinking that I had Parkinson's—I wasn't thinking anything. So you sort of say, "Gee, this is different. I guess I better find out everything I can about what the disease is about." So I did a lot of reading—and I decided to reject it, to put it out of my life. [Smiles.] But I wasn't angry or anything like that. What are you going to get angry about? I have a great excuse for my poor putting now. Phil Mickelson just misses 'em. I miss 'em for a reason.

ZALESKI: And Betty's reaction?

GARVEY: Acceptance. I think to some extent, given our involvement with Lizzie's autism, it kind of puts you in a frame of mind where you just deal with it. I mean, there's no use sitting around the saying, "Son of a bitch."

ZALESKI: Is there pain associated with it?

GARVEY: Not really. It was just an annoyance that the last two fingers on my hand weren't working very well. So now I sort of have to hunt and peck instead of using the computer the normal way. The biggest problem is that I do a lot of writing and it just takes more time now.

The funny thing is, those two fingers are now functioning better than when I was first diagnosed. And that's not supposed to happen. So who knows? There's no explanation for it. And I rarely have tremors in my hand—which is another symptom. Occasionally it happens, but not very often.

ZALESKI: How did they diagnose it—through a series of tests?

GARVEY: It's pretty much a physical thing, where they see how your joints are responding to moving around. They watch how you walk, for instance. One thing that happens with Parkinson's is that if you're walking, one arm doesn't swing like it normally does. So they can figure it out pretty easily.

ZALESKI: I know you still golf on occasion—I suspect you're not scoring as well?

GARVEY: Yeah, that's putting it mildly. I can still grip the club but my balance is off. So when I take the club back I'm not sure where it's going to come down. There are just too many things to think about to try to hit the ball properly. So I'm not hitting it well at all—not making good contact.

The first time I played in a while was this spring, when Betty and I went to visit friends in Phoenix. I said let's go out and play some golf—but if I fall into a sand trap, for Christ's sake, get me out. But now when I play, I only count how many good shots I hit. Total score doesn't matter. Someone asks, "How'd you play today?" "Oh, I had a good day—I hit six good shots." It's no longer, "I shot forty."

ZALESKI: What's the long-term prognosis?

GARVEY: Well, all the literature says it's progressive but isn't fatal. I mean, ultimately it's fatal, but when I talked to the neurologist he said I've probably got ten or fifteen years. So if I take the medications and do some exercise and so on, I've still got time. It's not like pancreatic cancer or some other disease where you've got six months to live.

But it's a degenerative disease—so golfing and just walking will become much harder. I do the treadmill for a half-hour every morning and that hasn't gotten harder yet—but it's boring. I've got some pain and stiffness when I wake up, but friends say, "What are you complaining about? I feel the same way. It's called arthritis." And it may well be. I'm at the age where you don't necessarily know what's causing it.

ZALESKI: Has it affected you mentally?

GARVEY: Ultimately it will—or probably will. About 50 percent of people who get Parkinson's eventually are affected mentally to some extent. I've already warned my neurologist that if he sees any indication that I'm becoming conservative he should up the dosage.

But one of the side effects is that you start to mumble—or you don't project your voice. So I went through a class in which you're coached on how to make sure you're speaking loudly and distinctly. You practice that.

I think where I notice it most is when I'm going to give a speech, I have to be better prepared than I used to. When I'm invited to give a talk about an issue, I have to be a little more organized. I can't speak off the cuff. And I find that I have a lot more trouble multitasking than I did just a few years ago.

ZALESKI: With all the advances in stem cell research, are you optimistic they'll find a cure for Parkinson's before your time is up?

GARVEY: Well, again, that's my hope. I went to this Parkinson's support group meeting the other day and this neurologist from the University of Wisconsin explained all the bad news about Parkinson's. He laid it all out. And finally I said, "Hey, excuse me, can we get to the good news now?" I pretty much knew all the bad stuff. I wanted to hear something encouraging.

But I must say attending these support group sessions where people talk about the disease—and I've been to three or four of them—does make it somewhat easier. And, of course, Betty's role in this is rather large.

But it's funny. When I'm with my kids, they tend to think there isn't anything wrong. Pam will say, "How was golf today, dad?" And I'll say, "What do you mean how was golf? It was crappy, how do you think it was? I can't play very well anymore." And she'll say, "Maybe you just need to play more." She doesn't see it because she's not with me every day.

ZALESKI: Has knowing that you have an incurable disease changed your perspective on life? For instance, do you find yourself thinking more about death and what happens after the final curtain falls?

GARVEY: [Smiles.] I don't have very many profound thoughts about that.

ZALESKI: Really? It seems that many people—if not most— practically become obsessed about death as they get older, especially if their health is deteriorating. You don't spend time pondering the meaning of life?

GARVEY: Actually, I did a very careful study of it and I concluded that you're going to go out of this game dead. It's just a question of when. No, I never really thought about it that much. There's nothing that indicates to me that there's a great big golf course upstairs where I can shoot sixty-five every time I tee it up.

ZALESKI: Do you believe in a hereafter?

GARVEY: Not really. I mean, if there is, there is. It's really one of those things where I don't think you should—at least from my perspective—spend a whole lot of time thinking about. What do we know anyway? Whatever happens, happens.

ZALESKI: Do you believe in God?

GARVEY: Oh, let's not get into that.

ZALESKI: You haven't dodged a single question in all of our sessions—but you're going to dodge this one?

GARVEY: Well, ok, there's something—I don't know what it is. I mean, in grade school I remember talking about infinity and how it always made me crazy. You'd ask your teacher, "Ok, the universe has always been?" Well, no, there was a big bang. "Ok, but what was here before the big bang?" Well, there was something. "What was it?" I mean, this universe is really pretty phenomenal. And you'd think, so it's always going to be here? How can that be?

ZALESKI: Einstein, I've read, believed there's a superior force responsible for the universe and life as we know it, but that the human brain isn't capable of figuring out what it is.

GARVEY: Well, if Einstein couldn't figure it out, some kid from Burlington, Wisconsin, sure as hell can't!

Epilogue

What was it about Ed Garvey that was so captivating, that caused him to stand out from the crowd? I posed that question to seven people who knew him well and asked each one if they would contribute a short, personal account of what he was like in private—warts and all—and why they valued his expertise and friendship. Here are their stories.

Dave Zweifel,
editor emeritus of *The Capital Times*

Ed Garvey and I were both born in 1940 and ended up at the University of Wisconsin in Madison at the same time.

Strangely, we didn't know each other even though we were both in ROTC. My student activism was confined to the Young Democrats, becoming secretary in the 1959–60 school year. That coincided with the 1960 Wisconsin presidential preference primary featuring John F. Kennedy and Hubert Humphrey. Now that was pure political excitement.

Ed's roommate was a guy named David Sheridan, who happened to be president of the Young Dems at the time. Still, Ed and I never met. He was off to bigger things, not only getting elected president of the Wisconsin Student Association but becoming president of the national association as well, a position that opened many doors for him in his young life.

We finally did link up in 1983 after he left the National Football League Players Association, where he had ticked off football fans by leading the players out on two strikes but had freed the players from what was essentially legalized slavery, forever changing professional football. I had just become the editor of *The Capital Times*, the newspaper that was founded to help the political career of a Wisconsin political icon known as "Fighting Bob" La Follette, and Ed had been named the deputy to attorney general Bronson La Follette, none other than Fighting Bob's grandson.

I guess you could say it was a good fit.

He and Bronson had a falling out within a few years, but in the interest of keeping Wisconsin progressivism alive that was undoubtedly a good thing. For after he was freed from the constraints inherent in helping run the state's highest law enforcement agency, it was no-holds-barred from there on. I managed to go along for a lot of the ride.

Others in Rob Zaleski's book will recount Ed's many accomplishments and remember his organizing skills and awesome wit that made this man a legend in his own time. I remember most of them, but I've got a couple of my own to share.

After leaving the attorney general's office, he started his own Madison law firm, of course, but it was much more than that. Early on he added a "division" to the firm he called Labor

Strategies Inc., a seat-of-the-pants effort to capture video of political events that could be used by progressive and pro-labor candidates in their election ads, for instance. His favorite venue was, of course, the State Legislature. He'd send the young video staffers to record the antics, especially of Republican legislators who routinely fought any bill that hinted of progressive thought.

I don't think I ever saw him happier than the day his video crew caught an astonishing meltdown on the assembly floor by then-Republican leader David Prosser, who became upset when the assembly speaker ruled him out of order while attempting to debate a health care bill. Prosser threw a monster tantrum, including a screaming fit while pounding and slapping the speaker's podium. Ed made sure that the video was widely distributed, and years later when Prosser was on the State Supreme Court he revived it to show that a report of Prosser losing his temper and trying to choke fellow justice Jane Walsh Bradley was perfectly in character.

Ed was never content to just argue cases in court or appear at legislative hearings on behalf of clients. He led confrontations to champion their causes, like the time he marched with hundreds of workers from a Waukesha printing plant, video cameras in tow. The plant had announced that it was closing down. The workers believed a bill pending in the state senate would save their jobs by forcing the printing firm to give new owners a chance. They wound up cornering GOP Majority Leader Mike Ellis in his office, and the video captured the desk pounding and tough language that ensued. The workers shut down the senate for eleven hours, but, unfortunately, the Republican senators held firm.

It was incidents like these when I realized befriending Garvey had changed my life forever. He'd call on a minute's notice and insist that I need to come and witness this in person.

He'd organize sessions of a "People's Legislature" that would "pass" campaign finance bills to take money out of politics or to declare that Supreme Court elections be funded by the public, not moneyed interests. And he took me along on the wild ride to organize Fighting Bob Fest, convincing me to persuade our charitable arm, the Evjue Foundation, to help underwrite it.

No, you didn't just get to know Ed Garvey, you had join him. He made sure of that.

Now that I think of it, good thing I didn't know him in college, I'd have never graduated.

Barbara Lawton,
Garvey's 1998 lieutenant governor running mate

I had just lost my first run for office, for state senate, in 1996. After that close look at the seedy underbelly of our political system, I decided I would never enter that arena again until we addressed the issue of money in politics.

Enter Ed Garvey into my life. Governor Thompson named a Blue Ribbon Commission to study campaign finance reform, and Ed countered by assembling "The Citizens Commission for a Clean Elections Option," chaired by former Chief Justice Nate Heffernan. My fresh expertise in elections got me an invitation to join, and I appreciated the chance to learn from a scrappy, strategic genius lessons that bold is better, integrity can carry the day, and the people will respond to a compelling invitation to engage in their democracy.

Crowds gathered to testify for the Heffernan Commission's public hearings, which became an emboldened base for a run for governor. Next move on Ed's chessboard: ask me to run with him, run as a team and promise to govern as a team. I never again wanted to spend endless hours on the phone begging for money, but Ed's vision for this race was to make money the issue, limit contributions to $100 as a contrast to the $10,000 limit for Tommy, and thus be free to travel the state with a campaign that would educate and invite the public to insist theirs was the special interest elected officials ought to heed.

So far so good. Ed's creative genius in the design of the campaign, loyal old friends and new volunteers drawn to his high energy and sharp wit, and Betty's permission, were enough to fuel an impressive launch to the Garvey/Lawton campaign. And then there were new lessons to learn: Ed's unflinching commitment to justice, combined with his self-proclaimed Irish temperament ("Is this a private fight or can anyone join?"), could get him into trouble. As we set off to nail down traditional Democratic support, he asked me to head over to meet with officers at the AFL-CIO. I blanched. Me, alone? Surely they would insist on dealing with the top of the ticket. And then the story came out that Ed had an active lawsuit against them, suing on behalf of a former union officer, now disabled and with some claim no one else had the courage to pick up. Seriously? He was running for governor while suing the AFL-CIO?

That moment opened a glimpse into the complexity of this man. He had hard edges honed by being driven to always do the "right" thing, his outrage could get dangerously close to self-righteousness, and his combative—and usually successful—negotiating style could unnecessarily undercut his statesmanship. His gift for stirring oratory, coupled with political passion and razor-sharp wit, drew cheering crowds and could lead him into trouble on occasion. And any of us who have ever been close to him can tell a story of how he threw a grenade into our relationship and kept on going. No apology needed when you're right. And no need to linger over past wounds when there's great work ahead. And on we would go.

There are endless riotous stories of that '98 campaign. We had a serious mission, but it was serious fun along the way. What could be more fun than, in the end, having some analysis credit your campaign with putting an end to Tommy's presidential aspirations? Or building a tremendous team of bright young people who learned organizing from the best and attached to the idea that holding forth a bold vision of justice could launch a movement?

Ed went on to lead movements to keep Perrier Inc. from draining Wisconsin's precious water supply and mining companies from destroying sacred land, to lead development of Fighting Bob Fest that helped underwrite a launch to Bernie Sanders's powerful presidential campaign. And those young people who gave their all to the Garvey/Lawton campaign and were confident we would win, whose pride in a soaring effort on behalf of our state dissolved into tears on election night, have all gone on to be strong leaders in their own realms.

No one could be more fiercely partisan and more objectively critical of his party than Ed. No one so passionately political and more dedicated to his family. He loved them beyond words. But, for instance, when Dave Zweifel and Ed and I would have our monthly lunch to take on the issues of the day, if I inquired about the family he would snarl and say, "Let's get back to business!"

Ed, a man driven by his love of family and justice, lifted into our lives by his immeasurable gifts and burdened by an uncompromising understanding of right and wrong. Incomparable and irreplaceable.

Mike McCabe,
former executive director
of the Wisconsin Democracy Campaign

I got to know Ed when he was running for governor in 1998, and I appeared with him at a few events. But I didn't really get to know him well until I helped with the planning for Fighting Bob Fest.

It's true that Ed intimidated a lot of people, and he had the famous Garvey temper, but he was actually pretty easy on me. I think he respected the work I was doing at the Wisconsin Democracy Campaign, specifically how money was ruining politics. However, I was often on the receiving end of the stinging Garvey wit. He poked fun at me a lot, about my appearance, my speaking style, even about the work I was doing on campaign finance reform, calling it my crusade or whatever. Even when he introduced me at Fighting Bob Fest and other venues, he'd make light of that work, even though I knew he valued it greatly.

But it never bothered me all that much, because I felt it was coming from a place of affection. I never once thought he was trying to put me down or belittle me—or that he was expressing anger. When we worked together, which was quite often, I'd see his temper from time to time, but he never unloaded on me. I don't know why that was, but if we didn't see eye-to-eye on something, we'd hash it out and move on to something else.

Why was I drawn to him? Well, I always felt like we were kindred spirits in the sense that we shared this belief that Wisconsin was better than the cronyism and the corruption that was seeping into our political system. He saw the evolution of our political culture and the role that big money was playing, and he was disturbed by it. I saw that same evolution and felt exactly like he did. I think we both took great pride in Wisconsin once being known as a beacon of clean, open, and honest government, and I think it broke both of our hearts to watch Wisconsin's reputation being tarnished.

I always felt that Ed was on the right side of most fights, and he had a magnetism about him, which is why he had such a significant following. So I felt like we could be good teammates and that I could help him reach more people than he was reaching—and vice versa.

I knew Ed the better part of twenty years, and the first five years or so it was strictly professional. But then it evolved into a friendship—to the point where he'd call me and ask if I wanted to go out for a grilled cheese sandwich, and we'd just shoot the breeze and enjoy each other's company. He had closer friends, people who were more his age, like Dave Zweifel, but we still had a lot in common, believed in a lot of the same things.

I'm not sure what the public's image of Ed was, but he wasn't much different in private. He had a tremendously sharp wit, which came through in his public appearances, but he was a prickly character, too. And privately, if he didn't respect somebody or care for them, he could be a little cruel. I remember him telling me a story about when he debated Bob Kasten while running for the U.S. Senate [in 1986], he made a remark to Kasten about his sex life, or something like that, right before the debate started, just to try throw him off, just to get under his skin. And, you know, that's something I would never do, it's something I don't have in me. But Ed had it in him. He could be really caustic—even if he respected you and admired the work you were doing.

I don't have any big gripes about that, but I'll give you an example of how Ed could be. He once lined me up to be a main stage speaker at Fighting Bob Fest. And that ended up becoming a tradition—he asked me back year after year. But this particular time, he had lined up John Conyers, the congressman, to speak on the main stage as well. Ed told me to plan on speaking for about twenty minutes. Well, unbeknownst to me, Conyers apparently showed up and told Ed he was pressed for time and needed to speak sooner. So Ed had people hold up signs while I was speaking that said, "Five minutes."

I had just started speaking when I saw the signs and assumed it meant I'd been talking for five minutes and still had fifteen minutes to go. But next thing I know, Ed is on the stage and giving me the look—and I realize what's happening. So I just turned to him and said, "Let me get out of this gracefully and pretend like it's a natural ending." So I quickly ended my speech and got off the stage, but it was not a nice thing to do to someone. There was no warning—I just sort of got the hook.

But Ed never apologized, never even acted as if he thought it was rude. He probably figured he was the emcee for this event, he had to make sure everything went smoothly and he had this congressman who needed to get on a plane, so he did what he had to do. He never even explained the situation—I heard about it from others later on. Now, some people would get bent out of shape over something like that, but I just let it go. We both forgot about it and just moved on. There was no sense in making a federal case out of it because it was what it was and I had to adjust on the fly.

What kind of governor would Ed have been? I think he would have been a principled, progressive governor. I don't think he would have pulled any punches; he would have followed his heart. There would've been many strained relationships between the governor's office and the legislature. Sparks would have flown, and he would've needed somebody—a chief of staff or somebody else within the administration—who would've been good at smoothing things over with certain legislators and other officials. Because Ed didn't suffer fools gladly, and he did have that prickly side to him. And if he was convinced that he was right, it didn't really matter who was lined up against him. He was like a bull in a china shop on issues that really mattered.

Would he have been effective? I think some people would have tried to create a narrative that he was ineffective and didn't work with people well enough. I think there would've been a lot of frayed nerves and hurt feelings. But in the end I think he would've accomplished a lot. Simply because he would've been a governor of principle, and he wouldn't have been afraid to take risks or take some unpopular stands. Now maybe that meant he would've been a one-term governor. Because Ed wasn't the kind of guy who'd sit around thinking about all the things he needed to do if he wanted a second term.

Pat Richter,
former University of Wisconsin athletic director, NFL star, and a former member of the NFLPA's negotiating team

Being a member of the NFLPA's negotiating committee, I suppose I did see a side of Ed that others rarely saw. I wouldn't call him volatile. He was just very quick witted and a little sarcastic at times. But he drove the owners nuts because he was so bright and always ahead of them, and he'd come up with these little digs, which they obviously didn't appreciate.

We had Ed as executive director, and [Nick] Buoniconti and myself and Ken Bowman were all player reps at various stages of being in law school. So we'd take notes at the meetings, and you couldn't believe some of the things Ed would say. The owners were used to having people roll over for them and that wasn't Ed's M.O. at all. He'd go toe-to-toe with them and wasn't afraid of anybody, even as young as he was [thirty-one when he accepted the job as executive director].

Remember, these guys were pretty much the icons of pro football, but Ed didn't care if it was [Dallas president and general manager] Tex Schramm or [New York Giants co-owner] Wellington Mara. He loved getting under their skin. And then, of course, we also had to deal with [NFL commissioner] Pete Rozelle, and as a group they always tried to split us and intimidate us and get us to disagree with one another. But Ed was never fazed by any of it and always felt really comfortable and wanted us to leave everything in his hands. And, of course, he had [veteran labor negotiator] Leonard Lindquist behind him and [UW economics professor] Nate Feinsinger was a sounding board as well.

It's interesting, because even after I left pro football I had a great relationship with Ed. I ultimately ended up at Oscar Mayer, representing the management part of labor with the meat packers. It was almost as if I'd gone to the other side, and there were a lot of people at Oscar Mayer who looked at me like, can we really trust you? They knew I'd been a union guy during my NFL days. And sometimes Ed would come back to Madison and we'd go talk to Nate Feinsinger, and some of the ideas Ed came up with would scare the hell out of you from a management perspective. But as a player, you loved Ed, because you know he'd go to the wall for you.

There's no question Ed was frustrated that the media was overwhelmingly opposed to our union. How do I explain it? I think some of it may have been related to Marvin Miller [executive director of the Major League Baseball Players

Association], who did a lot of things that kind of revolution-
ized how union contracts were negotiated from a baseball perspective. I think the NFL owners were fearful of Ed doing the
same thing.

But another factor, I think, was that Pete Rozelle was the
commissioner, and his background was in public relations for
the Los Angeles Rams organization. And he was an expert at
working the media and always getting the media to see things
from the owners' perspective. He was so good at it that whenever we were in negotiations with the league, we'd put out a
press release and it never showed up anywhere, for whatever
reason. And yes, that was frustrating.

Another factor was the evolution of the Super Bowl and
how the league treated reporters who attended that event. I
mean, Rozelle made sure the media was wined and dined for
days leading up to the game. He was smart enough to treat the
media like royalty and give them free gifts and whatever, and
it was a big deal. And we always felt it affected the way the
media covered us. And yeah, Ed was upset about that. We all
were.

The fact is, the owners pretty much controlled the press
back then. But, frankly, I think it would be different today
with social media and Ed's magnetic personality. I'd think
he'd be a wonder today and be able to explain what's really
going on, and fans would see things a lot differently.

Bill Kraus,
political pundit and former communications director
for Wisconsin Republican Governor Lee Dreyfus

Ed and I crossed paths in the early eighties when I was in Lee
Dreyfus's governor's office and Ed was across the hall working for Bronson La Follette, the attorney general, who Lee

fondly greeted whenever he saw him as "my lawyer." The relationship between the offices was continuously cordial. Ed and I had what I would describe as a HiYa relationship.

Ten years later, when I was newly back from seven years in New York, Andy Moore was recruiting panelists for what would become Wisconsin Public Television's weekend show. The show appeared every Friday and ended with a pundit panel that tossed around the week's political events. Both Ed and I were in the original cast on those shows along with Bill Dixon and Margaret Lewis. As the years went on, the panel pool expanded by adding Tony Earl, Steve King, and even Charlie Sykes, the Milwaukee mouthpiece.

I immediately liked Ed, and he liked me. We probably disagreed on most of the issues of those days but never disagreeably or publicly. During the ten years the show aired, Ed started a weekly website on politics. He invited me to make a contribution every week.

I stayed pretty much on subjects where we agreed: process subjects like gerrymandering, money in politics, transparency, a primary system that had gone awry, and the like. When I strayed into more partisan territory, I'm sure he regretted it. But he gave me free rein and never edited or criticized. This was more than he gave to any Democrat who got crosswise on anything with him.

In retrospect, it occurs to me that most of Ed's bad relationships were intraparty at the time and probably forevermore. The people most likely to be on Ed's enemies list were the owners of NFL teams and Democratic incumbents who were more moderate than Ed was on anything and everything.

We didn't socialize all that much but we got to know and like Betty and saw the two of them regularly at symphony concerts for sure and elsewhere in town as well.

The last time I saw Ed, I joined him for lunch. When we got to his home to pick him up, he was on the phone with a former Green Bay Packer discussing something about a book he was in the process of writing about his life and times as executive director of the professional football players union. The subject of the book generally was protecting the physical well-being of the players of this collision game. I recall that he protested the move from grass to plastic football fields on the grounds that beyond being hard, they didn't drain well enough. Petri dishes for disease is what he called them.

Ed died before the book was published. I hope it is revived as a fitting memorial to Ed and a rebuke to those who ignored his warnings. [Bill Kraus, who was highly active until the end, died at his Madison home on December 14, 2018, after a bout of pneumonia. He was 92.]

John Nichols,
Washington correspondent for *The Nation*
and associate editor of *The Capital Times*

When a Minnesota college professor named Paul Wellstone was thinking about making a decidedly uphill bid for the U.S. Senate in 1990, he picked up a copy of *The Progressive* magazine and read an article by Ed Garvey, who had just lost a U.S. Senate race in Wisconsin.

Stories of losing campaigns for high office do not usually inspire others to enter the fray. But the article Ed had penned— a fierce indictment of the corrupting influence of big money in politics titled "It's Money That Matters: A Candidate Looks Back in Anger"—captured Wellstone's imagination. The 1995 book, *Mr. Wellstone Goes to Washington*, recounted how the professor's "eyes lit up" when he read Garvey's populist call to action. Wellstone began to think that "the time might be right for running against money."

It was.

Wellstone was elected to the Senate in 1990, in the same election that saw another friend and fan of Ed's, Bernie Sanders, get elected to Congress from Vermont.

Both Wellstone and Sanders were among a multitude of activists across Wisconsin and the United States who have credited Ed with showing them how to forge a new politics that combined progressive idealism and a populist demand for clean elections.

Ed Garvey never held elective office. Yet, his bids for the U.S. Senate and the governorship in Wisconsin framed a new politics that erased the barriers between grassroots activism and electoral politics. He envisioned a day when elected officials would spring from movements and make it their mission to implement the programs of those movements.

Ed was a movement man. A civil rights campaigner who went south in the early 1960s with the Student Nonviolent Coordinating Committee. A student activist who served as president of the National Student Association in the turbulent 1960s. A labor activist who was the first executive director of the National Football League Players Association. And a courtroom activist who as a lawyer and legal strategist organized the long struggle to apply antitrust laws to the NFL and won major concessions from the owners. He crusaded for environmental protection as a deputy attorney general of Wisconsin and then represented labor unions in their battles with multinational corporations.

In 1986, Ed's bid for a U.S. Senate seat representing Wisconsin drew national attention as he built a rainbow coalition campaign—inspired by the presidential bids of his friend and longtime collaborator on progressive causes, the Reverend

Jesse Jackson. Linking labor and environmental groups, urban workers and farmers, women's rights campaigners and the LGBTQ community into a mass-movement campaign, Ed secured the Democratic nomination. Mimicking the populist approach that his friend Jim Hightower used to win election as Texas Agriculture Commissioner in 1982, Ed appeared to be headed for the U.S. Senate when his opponent, Republican Senator Bob Kasten, launched a heavily funded smear campaign that lied about his challenger's background. Kasten, who was supported by millionaire campaign donors and special-interest groups from across the country, narrowly prevailed with what at the time was characterized as one of the bitterest campaigns in modern American history. Later, when faced with a libel suit, Kasten conceded that the free-spending attack-ad campaign was false.

Ed Garvey's reaction to his setback was to start organizing against the big money that paid for attacks ads. His groundbreaking articles for *The Progressive* still turn up in textbooks on politics and they still inspire progressive activists and campaigners.

Ed made his last run for public office in 1998, securing the Democratic nomination for governor of Wisconsin with a bid that accepted only contributions of $100 or less. With fellow campaign finance reformer Barbara Lawton as his running mate for lieutenant governor, Ed outlined a democracy program that inspired a new generation of activists in the state. He also drew enthusiastic support from Paul Wellstone, who campaigned at Garvey's side in small towns and cities across Wisconsin. Jesse Jackson showed up as well, touring African American churches in Milwaukee with the man who had been one of the most ardent supporters of the civil rights advocate's 1988 president bid.

Ed did not win, but he increased the Democratic share of the

vote by almost ten points and played a critical role in helping
Russ Feingold get reelected to the U.S. Senate and boosting a
young ally, Tammy Baldwin, in her bid for a U.S. House seat.

Baldwin recalled something that was especially true, and
especially important, about the man: "Ed understood how
important it was to pass on to the next generation our proud
progressive tradition in Wisconsin."

Ed's persistence and passion even earned him the regard of
the man he ran against in the 1998 contest. "On 100 issues, Ed
and I probably agreed on 25—if we were lucky," said former
Wisconsin Governor Tommy Thompson, a conservative Republican. "But he was such a great speaker, such a great writer.
I just respected him so much because, even when we didn't
agree, I knew I was debating someone who believed in what
he was saying and was so good at saying it."

Ed never sought another office, but he never stopped campaigning. A brilliant public speaker with razor-sharp wit and
storytelling skills that he credited to his Irish background, Ed
stormed across the state and nation as an impassioned advo-
cate for economic and social justice, criminal justice reform,
organized labor, environmental protection, women's rights,
gay rights, disability rights, and, above all, democracy. He became, as Wisconsin Congressman Mark Pocan put it, "a Wisconsin icon and a brilliant national champion of labor and progressive causes [who] laid down an admirable path to follow
for all of us who believe in fighting for the underdog."

Ed organized Wisconsin's annual Fighting Bob Fest
celebrations—named for former Wisconsin Senator Bob La
Follette—which over the years drew tens of thousands of
people to hear Sanders, Jackson, Hightower, and others, as
well as the grassroots activists Ed had inspired to organize
and win races with Garvey-style campaigns.

When Sanders was campaigning for president in Wisconsin, prior to the state's 2016 presidential primary, he spoke often of the inspiration he took from Garvey. "Ed Garvey is one of my heroes. He is someone I look up to," said the senator. "There were very few people who recognized the full extent of threat that money in politics posed to democracy. But Ed did. He raised the alarm and he fought back, and I can't tell you how much we owe him—for that, and for a lifetime of progressivism."

Mark Murphy,
president of the Green Bay Packers and former NFLPA
player rep for the Washington Redskins

I was a rookie with the Redskins in 1977 and became the team's player rep for the union in '79. That's the first time I met Ed, and it was the third year of the collective bargaining agreement. I loved working with him right from the start. Of course, with the NFLPA's headquarters being in DC, I had a chance to interact with him more than some of the other player reps.

I don't recall anything specific from that first meeting, just that he was still relatively young and captivating to listen to and how the things he was saying about the clubs and the owners really resonated with me and the other player reps.

He made everything fun—I guess that's the best way to describe it. He was great at bringing people together, and I don't think he gets the credit he deserves. Not even close. Just the vision he had and all the things he did for the players.

Look at what they have now. This was Ed's dream. People thought we were crazy when the players went on strike in 1982 and demanded a percentage of the league's gross [profits]. Our rallying cry was, "We *are* the game," which of course is true. Now the players do get a percentage of the gross and everybody views it as a great system that's working well for everybody. And it's mainly because of Ed.

He was one of the most engaging, outgoing people I'd ever met. And he had this sort of gallows-like sense of humor, where you'd be at your lowest point and he'd say something that would make you burst out laughing. As I said, it was fun serving alongside Ed, and to me that's what stood out in terms of his leadership ability. It's a very rare quality.

I'd kind of grown up around labor relations. My father was director of labor relations for a steel company in Buffalo, so I had an interest in working in labor relations, even though I knew there were risks. As Ed used to say, being a player rep was kind of like smoking cigarettes—it was dangerous to your health. We knew some of the owners would hold it against us and that there was a chance our careers would be shortened because of it.

And that's where I felt Ed did such a great job. All of the players—the player reps in particular—knew we were fighting for a cause bigger than ourselves. And that we were fighting not only for current players, but future players as well.

In the beginning, especially after he was named executive director in 1971, he was widely despised not only by the owners but by the fans and the media, too. I think it's because he was trying to turn the NFLPA into a legitimate union, and he was fighting for rights for the players that the owners knew would cost them money in the long run.

But when you look at it now, many of the things he fought for are accepted as basic rights today. Of course, players now have the right to become free agents when their contracts expire. We accept that today, but people tend to forget that wasn't the case before Ed was hired.

Those were difficult, challenging times. I heard that when Ed negotiated a new contract for the players in '72 and they had a preseason strike, one of the lessons he and the union members learned was that striking in the preseason doesn't apply as much pressure as striking during the regular season. But they got through that and won some improvements, and after that they focused on more significant changes that would really benefit the players. And that's when Ed came up with the concept of players getting a percentage of the gross—which they eventually got after strikes in 1982 and 1987 and filing an antitrust lawsuit. And I think it's ironic that that's what we have now, and yet nobody gives Ed credit for the system we have in place today.

I remember when we were getting towards the end of the strike in '82, when it was really hard keeping all the players together. Ed was working nonstop through that entire period, seven days a week, practically twenty-four hours a day. For the last month, all the players were staying together at a hotel in New York. It was almost like being in a bunker, and we were all tired and wanted it to be over. But Ed kept us together, and we ended up securing a much improved collective bargaining agreement. Those were trying times, but they were also memorable times. And it's a tribute to Ed that we stayed focused and got a lot of the things we wanted.

Why doesn't he get more credit? I think part of it, quite honestly, was that Ed was young, he was abrasive, he was pushing for change, he could be—I want to make sure I say this right—he had a . . . biting sense of humor. And I think when you put that all together, when he was on your side, he was fighting for you and you loved it. But if you were on the other side, I can see where the owners didn't think he was the most beloved person in the world.

There were other reasons, of course. Back then, there was this belief that professional football players didn't deserve big salaries for essentially playing a kids' game. A lot of people felt, they don't need a union, they're not downtrodden workers. They're professional athletes and they're already given special treatment. But we kept reminding people that the players *are* the game, and that did have an effect, I think.

Ed and I remained close, even after he left the NFLPA in 1983. I remember flying out to Madison—I'd never been there before—and staying at the Edgewater Hotel for a going away party for him. It was also his last player rep meeting. Twenty five years later I came to Wisconsin to become president of the Packers, and I've traveled to Madison many times and kept in touch with Ed. But then, unfortunately, his health started to decline and I didn't see him as much in his later years.

I did attend his funeral [in February 2017], because I owe a lot to him. And it's not just me: players across the league—past, present, and future—owe a lot to Ed. His achievements are a big reason players get the salaries that they do today.

Frankly, I think he should be in the NFL Hall of Fame. I don't think it's ever been mentioned, but he certainly deserves it.

Acknowledgments

Most writers who complete a book, I presume, are grateful for the encouragement they received along the way. That's especially true in my case, considering I began this project with seventeen in-depth interviews with Ed Garvey in 2011 and—after a pause of four years—didn't submit my final manuscript to the University of Wisconsin Press until October 2018.

Although Garvey was a widely known progressive crusader for much of his adult life, neither of us was sure at the beginning what the final product would look like or whether it would hold much appeal—even to Garvey's many disciples. And we were both ok with that. I'd always been intrigued by Ed Garvey and wanted to know more about his roots and how he evolved into one of the most fascinating individuals I'd ever met. And Ed figured that, at the very least, the interviews would serve as a welcome distraction from the disease that would eventually take his life.

Thankfully, several people I greatly respect were convinced from the start that the project had merit and pushed me to get the manuscript published. Among the most influential were:

Chris Murphy, who was city editor in my last few years at *The Capital Times*—one of the best, I might add—and is now its managing editor; Dick Jones, my longtime friend and former colleague at United Press International's Madison Bureau; Dennis Punzel, a fellow staffer at both the *Green Bay Daily News* and *The Capital Times*, who was also a guiding light and voice of encouragement during the ten years I toiled on my novel, *Searching for Sal*, which was published in 2012; and my wife, Cindy, my sounding board and trusted advisor throughout my career.

In addition, I'm grateful for the boost I got from Mike McCabe, former head of the Wisconsin Democracy Campaign and one of the most honest public figures I've known. McCabe, who was among the many able candidates who lost to Tony Evers in the 2018 Democratic gubernatorial primary, had grown close to Garvey in the final years of Ed's life. And he maintained during our brief meeting in the midst of his hectic campaign that my interviews with Ed not only would be appreciated by his ardent followers but would have great historical value as well.

To be sure, there were others who offered words of encouragement—too many to mention here. But they know who they are, and I want them to know they were a big reason I made it to the finish line.

But even with such unwavering support, this book wouldn't have been completed without the assistance of several loyal colleagues: Natasha Kassulke, manager of strategic communication for the UW vice-chancellor's office for research and graduate education and a part-time faculty member at Madison College, who helped me overcome my digital deficiencies and transform the manuscript into a presentable form; Samara Kalk Derby, my former *Capital Times* comrade, who caught an embarrassing number of typos and other errors—just as she'd done with *Searching for Sal*; and Dennis McCormick, the veteran librarian at Madison Newspapers, whose research skills on this project were invaluable.

I also want to thank Ed's wife, Betty, and their daughter Kathleen—an attorney, just like her father—for providing photos from the family albums that show the kid from Burlington at various stages of his life and, I believe, complement the interviews.

Finally, I'm grateful to Adam Mehring, the University of Wisconsin Press's managing editor, for his guidance and meticulous editing, and to Gwen Walker, the Press's executive editor, who never lost patience with this technophobe through the long and sometimes arduous process and whose enthusiasm for the manuscript was a constant source of inspiration.

Rob Zaleski is a freelance writer and award-winning columnist. He spent twenty-six years writing for *The Capital Times* in Madison during Ed Garvey's time as a political activist. Previously, as the sports editor at the *Green Bay Daily News*, Rob covered Ed's tenure as the executive director of the National Football League Players Association. Rob is the author of the novel *Searching for Sal* and his work has appeared in *Madison Magazine* and *Isthmus*.